Passover for Christian Tradition

By Susie Hawkins and Melanie Leach

Cover Table Design by TGFX Design Studio

Cover & Back cover Layout by Happy Services via fiverr Designs

Edited by Tanya Leach

Dedications

To my husband, Will, for supporting this passion to know more about the One who saved me. To my son, Nicholas, for always giving me a reason to smile.
- Melanie

To my husband, OS, for patiently (for the most part) answering my endless questions and encouraging me as I explored this topic. Also, I will forever appreciate my children and grandchildren for being so willing to come along on this journey with me.
- Susie

Table of Contents

Acknowledgements

We want to thank our Messianic Jewish friends who answered our many questions with joyful hearts and a spirit of unity in helping to give this book the Jewish "voice" it desperately needed. Thank you Karen Faith and Raoul Garcia with Way Cool Angels, Inc. Your hospitality, prayers and encouragement have helped propel this passion project of ours forward. Michelle and Grace - big hugs to you, too. We love you!

Melanie: I want to thank you, Susie, for joining me on this book adventure. I could not have had the courage to venture out and do this thing on my own. Your insight, prayers, study and theological acumen have helped make this book materialize. Your quick wit and spirit of fun has made this a great journey. Thank you!

Introduction

A Word from Melanie:
"How did a Baptist girl from South Louisiana end up studying the Jewish Passover? Are you becoming Jewish?" My aunt asked when I told her I was writing a book about Passover.

No, I'm not turning Jewish, although I do believe Christians have been "grafted" into the family of God as Paul describes in Romans 11. Ten years ago, our Jewish friends invited my husband and me to their family Passover Seder. I had never heard of a Seder but as a Christian, I had always been curious about my Jewish heritage. I was eager to experience Passover with them.

Now, when it comes to food, some have called me "picky" and not very adventurous. However, this was a turning point for my palate. I knew I couldn't be rude and needed to eat what was served, which would be traditional Jewish Passover foods. God gave me some kind of tongue-grace and I ate it. I ate it all and I loved it!

Upon arriving at our friends home, we nibbled appetizers of matzah (unleavened bread), chopped liver, an apple fruit mix called charoset, and horseradish. I figured out the matzah was my "cracker" that needed to be dipped in the other sides. We sipped kosher wine while we noshed on these traditional hors d'oeuvres and waited for sunset. Sunset is when the Seder would begin.

In the dining room the hostess placed booklets, called Haggadahs, at each place setting.

The booklet contained prayers, traditional sayings and bible readings and provided the order of the Seder. I admit I was a little nervous reading from this booklet since I was unfamiliar with the content.

Our friends led the Seder as Jewish families do and have been doing for thousands of years. The Seder retells the story of the Exodus, when God delivered His people, Israel, from slavery. As we each read and participated in this ancient tradition, I couldn't help but think about Jesus - the Lamb - He was IN this story even though He wasn't mentioned once.

Knowing Jesus participated in a Seder all the years of His life, including the night before his death on the cross made it even more meaningful to Will and me. It put us IN His story! The night before Jesus's death on the cross, while leading a Seder, Jesus said to his disciples in Luke 22:15, "I earnestly desire to eat this Passover with you tonight." He knew what would happen that very night and the next day, yet He kept the Passover Feast that night as he had all the years of His life. I was overwhelmed with the spiritual truths I was seeing and experiencing in the Seder.

Years later when Will and I hosted our first Passover Seder, I was seven months pregnant with our son Nicholas. We saw this as an opportunity to start a new tradition at Easter for our family. However, I wanted to bring Jesus into our ceremony and honor Him because I believe that was His original intention.

While researching for this book, Susie and I have had the privilege to meet some wonderful Messianic Jewish Believers. These are people of Jewish descent who are believers in Jesus - or Yeshua as the promised Messiah. They have been an incredible resource in helping us bring a Jewish "voice" to this book.

Jewish Believers have been conducting "Christian Seders" since the first century. This Seder we share with you originated with them - Jewish Believers in Yeshua. Our desire in writing this book is to bear good fruit and inspire Christians to embrace this tradition during Holy Week or sometime during the Easter season with friends, neighbors and family. Passover is so much more than just a feast celebrating Israel's exodus from Egypt. It's a multi-sensory expression of our Christian faith and heritage. It's the story of Redemption, and it all takes place around the table. STEP INTO THE STORY and Experience a NEW Easter Tradition.

A Word From Susie:
Our move from Oklahoma to south Florida in 1978 introduced us to a variety of new (and often puzzling) cultural experiences. One of those was living in an area that had a significant Jewish population. Our second grade daughter, Wendy, was attending an elementary school where probably half of her class was Jewish. The day before the winter break, the children performed skits and songs from their own tradition. The Christians kids sang "Silent Night," with Mary and Joseph in bathrobes and a baby doll wrapped up as baby Jesus. The Jewish children sang about "dreidles" and the Eight Days of Hanukkah, both completely foreign to me. Sitting at the back of Mrs. Mickler's

classroom at Peters Elementary, I felt strongly that I needed an understanding of Judaism. Yes, I wanted a better understanding of our Jewish friends and neighbors, but I also instinctively knew this was important as a follower of Jesus.

He was, after all, a first century Jew whose life and ministry was characterized by that faith. In time we met a couple who were "messianic Jews," believers in Christ as the promised Messiah. Their practices were Jewish, but they believed in Jesus as the promised Messiah. That spring our women's Bible study hosted the first "Christian Seder" I had ever seen, led by our messianic friends. I was fascinated. Christ was so clearly in this experience! The figurative language and metaphorical meanings of the foods, the liturgy, the prayers, all pictured the beautiful story of God's redemption of mankind. The messianic Seder is the story of all believers, but told from their unique viewpoint as God's chosen people. I was hooked.

In addition, my husband and I began taking groups to Israel every year and have continued to travel there on pilgrimages for the past thirty years. One of our greatest delights has been our long friendship with the Jaffe family, devout Jews, who so graciously invite us along with others to their Shabbat table when we are in Jerusalem (Shabbat is the Sabbath, a day of rest observed in Israeli culture). The energetic and stimulating dinner conversations flow from politics to religion to cultural issues and everything in between. The liturgy, music and prayers that surround the meal tell their story as God's chosen people. Returning to our hotel, as we walk through the quiet streets (no driving on Shabbat), I always have the same wistful feeling - a sadness that we as Christians have nothing in our culture that even remotely parallels the weekly Shabbat family dinner with no interruptions or distractions (or technology!) Our Jewish friends have a treasure in their Shabbats and festivals and we should learn from them.

Passover is a centuries-old Jewish tradition and practice. So why should Christians embrace it? I believe there are three reasons to do so. One, Jesus took the Passover with His disciples the night before He was crucified. It was at that dinner that He instituted the New Covenant, which according to Christian doctrine superseded the Old. It was there He held up the bread (matzah) as an illustration of His broken body, and the cup of wine that demonstrated His shed blood. Communion, or the Lord's Supper, is an ordinance of the church and is a memorial to Christ's sacrificial death. When we observe Passover during Holy Week from this perspective, we are stepping into His story, doing what Jesus did the night before His death.

Secondly, Passover was intended as a strategic way to teach the next generation about their faith history. This celebratory meal is a multi-sensory one with food, smells, music and interaction designed to interest all ages and include them in the story. As believers, this is a fresh approach to opening up spiritual conversations with the younger crowd. Third, Christianity has two major celebrations - Christmas and Easter. Christmas is packed with family traditions of foods, gifts, church services, parties, etc. But Easter is usually celebrated only at a church service and/or an Easter egg hunt. A family Seder held a week or two before Easter can demonstrate the gospel story in a fresh and creative way. The messianic community has celebrated Passover in this way for centuries and we are eager to expand their Seder into evangelical thought and practice.

One of my great joys has been doing demonstrations of the Passover Seder in my grandchildren's classrooms during Holy Week. I bring the foods and explanations, and their teachers provide pictures and any additional resources. Children can often grasp more than we give them credit for, and doing this is one of my highlights of the season.

The story of God's redemption of His people is the over-arching narrative of Scripture. From the first Passover to Jesus's final one and from our Lord's Supper observances to the Christian Seders of today - these stories all fit perfectly into His larger one. And remember, we are living between Christ's two comings. One day we will celebrate the full feast at God's own table, at the Marriage Supper of the Lamb, the culmination of history. But until then, retelling this story every year during Holy Week reinforces gospel truths and leads us to marvel again at the astounding grace of God. I am not just interested in the Christian Seder, but am compelled to observe it and share it with others. It brings such rich insights to our spiritual journeys as we anticipate Resurrection Day. It's a new Easter tradition. Will you join us?

BOOK I: UNDERSTANDING PASSOVER

Chapter 1: Christians & Passover? Isn't Passover A Jewish Thing?

Yes, Passover is a "Jewish thing", but it is also a "Christian thing!" The two are related. Jesus celebrated Passover all the years of His life, including the night before He died. It's our hope to show you how Passover can help make your Easter season more meaningful by allowing you to walk in Jesus's Jewish shoes. Passover is a wonderful, God-inspired tradition filled with insights relevant to you, as a believer and follower of Jesus. Simply stated, it serves as a picture of Jesus and His ultimate sacrifice as the Lamb of God who takes away the sins of the world. Today, we invite you to step into the story with your friends and family this Easter by celebrating Passover for Christians.

Christians celebrate two major events annually on the church calendar: Christmas (the birth of Christ) and Easter (the resurrection of Christ). Christmas observances are tied closely to home and church, with families having their own family traditions as well as attending Christmas services together. However, Easter is usually only observed in a church service. Many families have an Easter meal together, but in our busy and fractured culture, even that may not happen.

Passover for Christians provides an opportunity for families to share a meal together during or prior to Holy Week (the week before Easter), and step into the final week of Jesus's life, His death and resurrection. Passover enables us to pause and observe His death in preparation for Easter Sunday. Good Friday and Easter

– or Resurrection Sunday – is the crux of our Christian faith and heritage. However, over time this season has been downgraded in our culture to a "Happy Spring," "Easter Bunny," and candy-egg sort of event. While the church still emphasizes Easter (hopefully), Americans in general have lost sight of its true meaning. While these other practices may be harmless, they distract from the very reason for the Easter celebration, which is the bodily resurrection of our Savior, Jesus Christ, the Son of God. It is time to recapture the wonder and rich tradition of this season, beginning with Passover, a purposeful meal around the dinner table.

We understand that no one needs another event to add to their busy schedules, but sharing the Christian Passover with friends and family will enrich your season like nothing else. By connecting Passover, Holy Week and Easter, we bridge the Old and New Testaments and can see the overarching theme of God's redemptive acts on behalf of His people. Passover and Easter – it's not "either or" it's "both."

The early Jewish disciples celebrated Passover. This is supported historically by studies conducted of the traditions and beliefs of the Jewish people during the Second Temple period (530 BC – 70 AD.) It's important to note that "Christian" does not necessarily mean "gentile." People of Jewish descent who believe in Jesus are Christians too. In fact, most Christians for the first decade or so after the death and resurrection of Jesus, were Jewish. (Today they are referred to as "messianic Jews", meaning they believe in Christ as their Messiah, but have not ceased being Jewish.)

The Christian observance of Passover was well established before the Jewish Diaspora (the scattering of the Jewish people into the Mediterranean world after Rome destroyed Jerusalem in 70 AD). Many gentiles also welcomed the gospel message and practiced the Jewish feasts including Passover. There has never been a time in the history of the church when there was not some degree of a Jewish-Gentile presence. So, believers have a connection with Passover, even though we may not realize it. This perspective is important as we explore the Seder and its relationship to Christianity.

If you grew up in an evangelical church you know how important the imagery of "blood" is - such as the blood of the Old Testament sacrifices, the blood of the lamb, being "washed in the blood," covered by the blood and the blood of Jesus. This is because the Bible says without the shedding of blood there is no forgiveness of sins (Hebrews 9:22). We are sinners and in need of a savior, a substitute, someone who can take our place and punishment for this sin. In the Old Testament, the sacrifices for sin were innocent animals offered up in the place of the person or people. These temporary sacrifices looked forward to the time when God would provide the true sacrifice, the Messiah who would one day make all things right between us and God. The New Testament revealed Jesus as the Lamb of God who takes away the sins of the world once and for all. By believing in Him, we are saved.

Melanie:
The first time I hosted our Christian Passover Seder, it took all day for me to prep the food and set the table.

My husband, Will, and I decided to hold our Passover on the Thursday night before Good Friday. I was working at that time so I took that Thursday off to get the house and food ready. Our dining room table seated eight people, so I invited ten people, thinking some would drop out – which they did so we had a perfectly full table of seven. We had no idea what we were doing, but we were among friends who didn't know either. This is the great thing about friends and neighbors - even when you don't know them very well. You'll certainly get to know them after hosting a Passover Seder - especially that first time. After it was finished, we all agreed that it felt like something special just happened around our table. Our conversations were all about God and how good He was, we were discussing deep things of the Bible and linking the Old Testament with the New. It was all about Jesus and the cross. We shared the gospel that night and had a really good time doing it.

Susie:
My first exposure to a Christian Seder was with Messianic Jewish friends, Neil and Jamie Lash. I had no earthly idea of the link between Passover and Jesus, and I was captivated the first time I experienced it. Their teaching made the Christian/Jewish connection so clear! After our first visit to Israel, I began to put it all together – our Jewish heritage, the Passover and sacrifices, the prophecies about Christ, His death – it all began to make sense as a larger story. In sharing this experience over the years I continue to marvel at God's ways and am so eager to share the richness of the Christian Seder with others.

What Does This Have To Do With Me? I'm Under Grace, Not The Law

The Passover Seder for Christians allows us to experience the story of redemption as told throughout the Bible. Jesus celebrated the Passover during His lifetime as an observant Jew, and was sharing the Passover meal with His disciples the night before He was crucified. At that meal He instituted the Lord's Supper while taking the bread and wine. Since we know "the rest of the story," we fully understand the rich symbolism that Jesus set forth at that Passover meal we call the Last Supper.

The Seder not only puts us into Jesus's story, but also into the over-arching story of redemption. Passover looks back on God's miraculous deliverance of His people from Egyptian slavery, which brought them freedom. When Jesus instituted the New Covenant at the Lord's Supper, He was demonstrating God's redemptive plan and purpose for His people. Today, we observe the Lord's Supper (communion), as a way of commemorating His death and burial.

The Passover observance is the way God chose to instruct His people to teach their children. Throughout history, Jews have used the Passover Seder to teach younger generations about their long and legendary history. As Christians, we want to follow their lead and do the same. In God's own words:

"Obey these instructions as a lasting ordinance for you and your descendants. When you enter the land that the Lord will give you as he promised, observe this ceremony. And when your children ask you, 'What

17

does this ceremony mean to you?' then tell them, 'It is the Passover sacrifice to the Lord...'" (Exodus 12:24-27, NIV).

The gospel message, illustrated through the Seder meal, is an extraordinary way to teach children and others spiritual truths. Using this "immersive" approach is an effective way to pass on knowledge. By using all five senses, we are better able to grasp the meaning of symbols and Biblical truths.

A Jewish Perspective On Passover

Passover has significance to the Jewish people that we as gentiles can easily miss. The message of "freedom" and "deliverance" speaks to their souls like nothing else. If we look at their history, we can see why. The Jews consider Genesis 12 to be the "deed" to their land, Israel. God gave it to them, in order that they might live in freedom as His covenant people, worshiping Him according to their traditions and beliefs while flourishing as a nation. However, throughout their history they have been periodically separated from their land and singled out for destruction, particularly after the Jewish Diaspora in 70 AD. This longing to live free from oppression and violence has been a part of the Jewish mindset for centuries. From the Egyptian bondage, to the Babylonian exile, to the violent anti-Semitism of the medieval and reformation ages, to the 19th and 20th century Jewish pogroms (organized massacres) in Eastern Europe and Russia, to the Holocaust and present day, the Jews have fervently prayed for freedom and safety from those who would destroy them.

In his book *The Battle for Israel's Soul,* Daniel Gordis tells about the father of Menachem Begin, one of the greatest leaders of the Zionist movement (a movement that promoted the establishment and development of the state of Israel). According to Begin, one of the most emotional memories of his childhood was his family's Passover Seder. At the end of the meal, when the liturgy read, "Next year in Jerusalem", his father would hold his head in his hands and weep, desperately praying for a place where his people and his own children could live and worship, free from oppression and the scourge of anti-Semitism. This account (undoubtedly repeated around thousands of Jewish tables), demonstrates this centuries old longing of the Jewish soul. The words of HaTikvah, (The Hope), the national anthem of Israel, describe it this way:

"As long as the Jewish spirit is yearning deep in the heart,
With eyes turned toward the East, looking toward Zion
Then our hope – the two thousand year hope – will not be lost.
To be a free people in our land,
The land of Zion and Jerusalem"[1]

"Next year in Jerusalem,"[2] which is part of the Seder's concluding liturgy, does not mean a trip or tour to Israel. It's so much more than that - it refers to their dream of being a free people, safely living in or returning to the land that God gave them so many centuries ago. To the Jewish heart, the deliverance theme of Passover is the embodiment of their faith, their hope and their prayers.

The Jewishness Of Christianity

As Christians, it's crucial that we understand our spiritual roots are Jewish. The Jews gave us our Scripture, our history and our theological distinctions as the people of God. Jesus ("Yeshua" in Hebrew) was a descendent of King David as well as a faithful observer of Jewish law and practice. Jewish believers in Christ, point out the parallels (based upon numerous New Testament scripture passages), symbolism and differences between these two faiths. Because of God's covenant with Abraham, we Gentiles are blessed (see Genesis 12:1-3). We are participants in the blessings that come from the Jewish covenant. Ephesians 3:6 says: "Gentiles are fellow heirs and fellow members of the body, and fellow partakers of the promise in Christ Jesus through the gospel." As far as Passover, the Seder originated with and belongs to the Jewish people. We, as followers of Christ, are grateful to share in its blessings and in "this night that is different from all other nights."[2]

Our Jewish friends who are believers, referring to Passover, have asked us, "What took you guys so long to realize the Seder is for you, too?!"

Did You Know?

"Hear, O Israel: The Lord our God, the Lord is one. Love the Lord your God with all your heart and with all your soul and with all your strength. These commandments that I give you today are to be on your hearts. Impress them on your children. Talk about them when you sit at home and when you walk along the road, when you lie down and when you get up. Tie them as symbols on your hands and bind them on your foreheads. Write them on the doorframes of your houses and on your gates." (Deuteronomy 6:4-9, NIV)

This passage is called "The Shema," (shu-MAH), the central prayer of Judaism, and is usually the first passage a child memorizes. It is the foundation of Jewish faith and practice. The Shema to Jewish people is like John 3:16 is to Christians.

Chapter 2: What IS Passover?

The story of the first Passover is one of the epic dramas of the Bible. It begins in Exodus 1, with Jacob's sons moving their families and all their possessions to Egypt because of the devastating famine in Canaan. Their brother, Joseph, whom they had sold into slavery years earlier, had providentially risen to a powerful, political position in Pharaoh's government. Through Joseph's intervention, his father, brothers and their families relocated to Egypt, escaping starvation in Canaan.

However, years passed and a new dynasty arose in Egypt, a king who did not honor the relationship the previous Pharaoh had with Joseph's extended family. The Israelite population had exploded, and the new ruler was fearful of their sheer number and the potential for trouble. His solution was to force them into slavery, in order to construct his building projects. Ironically, the more the Israelites were oppressed, the more numerous they became.

Eventually Pharaoh commanded all baby boys to be thrown into the Nile, his way of managing the population growth. Exodus 2 opens with the backstory of the Israelites' future deliverer, Moses, who would one day lead them out of Egypt and into freedom (read Moses' story in Exodus 2-3).

The Israelites were in Egypt for approximately four hundred years (see Exodus 12:41), and the time had finally come for their liberation. God chose Moses to be their leader and used him to communicate His purposes to pharaoh and Egypt as God, Himself began the process of freeing Israel by sending ten plagues of judgment upon the Egyptians:

- The Nile was turned into blood
- Frogs
- Lice
- Flies
- Death of livestock
- Boils
- Hail
- Locusts
- Darkness
- Death of the firstborn in each family.

The Israelites were spared the first nine plagues; however, in accordance with the last plague, Israel was required to act. God instructed His people on how they could escape this final judgment – the death of the firstborn child – on their own families, as well as prepare for their hurried exit from Egypt. Each family was to take a lamb, kill it and spread the blood over the doorposts of their home. The death angel would then "pass over" each of their homes and their firstborn children spared (Exodus 12:13). They were also to roast and eat the lamb, and prepare bread that could be quickly baked (without leaven). That fateful night the firstborn children of the Israelites were spared, but the Egyptians, including Pharaoh, lost their firstborn children. Pharaoh demanded the Israelites leave immediately, and they quickly departed under Moses' leadership, taking food, livestock and other necessities. After a miraculous escape from Pharaoh's army through the Red Sea, they wandered in the Sinai desert for forty years until entering Canaan, the "Promised Land."

While in the wilderness, the Israelites observed Passover annually (see Numbers 9:1-4). It would be an ordinance, an annual ceremonial meal that would remind them of God's deliverance out of slavery. Since that time – almost 3,300 years later - Jews in every culture have observed Passover.

How Does This Relate To Christians?

Traditionally, the church has seen the Passover Feast as the foreshadowing of Christ's atonement on the cross. The Old Testament feasts were "pictures" or "shadows" of the real event that would take place at God's appointed time (see Colossians 2:17). Christ, the Messiah, the sinless Son of God, would freely give His life in our place, taking on God's punishment for sin and providing our salvation. Christ, as the sacrificial lamb, would enable us to be reconciled with God, become part of His family, and rest eternally secure in His love.

This was the view of first century believers, and one of the New Testament's most prominent themes. For example: John the Baptist identified Jesus as the "Lamb of God, who takes away the sin of the world!" (John 1:29, NIV), using the imagery of the sacrificial lamb (Exodus 12:3). For the Jews, John's meaning would be clear. The blood of the Passover lamb spread over the doorposts of each home brought deliverance from death, just as Jesus's blood would do. This theme of Christ as the Passover, or sacrificial lamb, is woven into the theology of the New Testament.

In Acts 8:26-27, Philip explained the gospel to an Ethiopian who was puzzled as he read Isaiah 53:7-8. He identified Jesus as the innocent lamb, "led to the slaughter." In Revelation, the title of the victorious Christ is "The Lamb" (see Revelation 5:8-13). Paul wrote in 1 Corinthians 5:7: "For Christ, our Passover [lamb] has been sacrificed" Also Colossians 2:17: "These [festivals, Sabbaths] are a shadow of the things that were to come; the reality, however, is found in Christ."

Passover points to Jesus, who fulfilled every point of the law and every prophecy regarding the coming Messiah. The Old Testament Passover story and its metaphorical meanings relate to Christianity in powerful ways! Believers who celebrate the Christian Seder can help explain these meanings and the Biblical word pictures with others around the table.

Another view of Passover is how it relates to believers through the Lord's Supper and the Marriage Supper of the Lamb. Jesus hosted and led a Passover meal with His disciples on the night before His crucifixion, when he instituted the Lord's Supper, the sign of the New Covenant. Communion is one of the two ordinances of the church, and is how we remember His death in accordance with 1 Corinthians 11:26.

In Revelation 19:7-9, John refers to the "Marriage Supper of the Lamb", the celebratory feast for all believers who are finally at home with their Lord. This banquet will be the culmination of all history. The Lord's Supper looks forward to this meal at the end of the age. After drinking the cup, Jesus said, "I will not drink of the fruit of the vine from now on until that day, when I drink it new with you in My Father's kingdom" (Matthew 26:29, NIV). We are currently between feasts – the Lord's Supper and the Marriage Supper of the Lamb. We will take a closer look at these connections in the following chapters.

Passover Key Themes And Christian Connection

1. Israel was called out by God as His chosen people to be separate from the world.

Just as the Israelites were chosen by God to be His people, believers in Christ have been chosen. "For He chose us in Him before the creation of the world to be holy and blameless in His sight. Because of His love for us He predestined us for adoption to sonship through Jesus Christ, in accordance with His pleasure and will." (Ephesians 1:4-5, NIV). We have been called out of the world, if you will, and placed into Christ's family – the church, in Him. "In Him we were also chosen, having been predestined according to the plan of Him who works out everything in conformity with the purpose of His will, in order that we, who were the first to put our hope in Christ, might be for the praise of His glory" (Ephesians 1:11-12, NIV). The apostle Peter confirms this when he says in I Peter 2:10, "Once you were not a people, but now you are God's people; once you had not received mercy, but now you have received mercy." Salvation has come to the world in Jesus. You have been chosen.

2. They were called to remember what God did for them. He saved them with a mighty hand.

God instructed the Israelites to observe Passover annually in order to remember His deliverance out of Egypt. In the same way, Jesus tells his disciples to eat the bread and drink wine to remember His death and our deliverance from sin. Both of these meals were intended as memorials. The apostle Paul emphasized the significance of this in 1 Corinthians 11:26: "For whenever you eat this bread and drink this cup, you proclaim the Lord's death until He comes." The Lord's Supper is a reminder of Christ's sacrificial death that bought us our salvation just as the Passover is a reminder of God's deliverance from Egyptian bondage.

3. They were to tell the story to each generation.

Our obedience is crucial in telling the biblical story of redemption and deliverance to the generations who come after us. Just as Jewish families have observed Passover for nearly 3,300 years, the church has observed communion since the first century. By maintaining this practice and by understanding and teaching its rich symbolism, we share Jesus's story and our stories with the next generation.

Jesus did not ask believers to remember His death in liturgy, music or art, but through a MEAL around a TABLE among friends, future-friends and family. When we remember God's faithfulness in our past, it gives us more confidence to believe Him now and in his future promises. His words were true for Israel at Passover in the Old Testament; His words were true at the Last Supper. We can trust His promise for the future, that

He IS coming back as a conquering King of Kings and Lord of Lords. One day, we will feast with Him at His table where He is the Host!

Personal Passover Stories

"We had a Passover to remember. With no festive food, no silver candlesticks and no wine - with only our simple desire to connect with God - we had a holiday more profound than any we have known since. I thank God for allowing me to live to be able to tell my children and grandchildren about it. Even more, I feel obligated to the younger generations of my family, who never experienced what I did, to pass on the clarity it gave me - the vivid appreciation of God's presence in my life, of His constant blessings, wonders and teachings... and of His commitment to the survival of the Jewish people." (Amelie Jacobovits remembering Passover as a young child in 1941 when she and three children were separated from their parents and hidden by a local farmer in a barn in Nazi occupied France) [3]

"The whole evening was a beautiful experience with Christian friends and strangers. All of this culminated in fellowship and taught each of us that we too can learn something new – that is very old. It was truly a community effort and event." (Virginia Haynes, Passover 2014 in Dallas, TX) [4]

"We started celebrating Passover over 15 years ago, long before we even met Jewish people and it has become a standard part of our Christian experience and tradition. It started with the realization that early Christians practiced it, and I didn't know what it was.

So, I studied the issue and began factoring it into our lives, and it has meant the world to us.

Every year, we try to invite new guests so someone new can experience it. Some years ago, I made a crown of thorns and got a large nail. Before we partake of the third cup, we pass the nail and the crown around the table for each to personally hold and think about what the Savior did for us. My understanding is the "passing of the nail" is an old European Easter tradition. It has added great meaning to our Passover." (Ruben Barrett)[5]

"We enjoy celebrating not only the rich history of God's saving the Israelites and bringing them out of slavery. It helps us to usher in Easter with a renewed perspective and is something that we look forward to every year." (Dawn Zapata)[6]

Did You Know?
Other traditions, like the "Cup of Elijah" and "Miriam's Cup" have been added to Passover Seders over the years. Elijah's Cup is in reference to the prophecy in Malachi 4:5 which states that Elijah will come before the Messiah to announce His coming. In Jewish homes, the host sets an extra place setting for Elijah at the table. At a designated time during the Seder, the children go to the door and open it for Elijah to come in and announce that the Messiah has come. We acknowledge this tradition in our Christian Passover; however, we discuss Jesus's words in Matthew 11:14 regarding John the Baptist and that he was the "Elijah" who announced Jesus as Messiah.

"Miriam's Cup" is a fairly new tradition created in the 1970s. She was the sister of Moses and played a prominent part in Jewish life while in the desert forty years. Jewish tradition teaches that a miraculous "well" accompanied the Hebrews throughout their journey in the desert, providing them with water. It is said that God gave this well to Miriam, to honor her bravery and devotion to the Jewish people. Households who add Miriam's Cup do so to acknowledge the role of virtuous women in Jewish households and history. Her cup is placed beside the Cup of Elijah. We like this tradition because Paul mentions a "spiritual rock" that gave Israel water in the desert in I Corinthians 10:1-5, referring to Christ.

These traditions, shared experiences and stories help bring Passover to life and make your Seder your own. As you become more comfortable hosting Seders, you will start your own traditions and introduce your own stories that glorify the Lord, reminding you of His faithfulness.

Chapter 3: Passover Seder? What's That?

Despite being scattered across the world since 70 AD, the Jewish community has maintained its unique heritage. The Hebrew language, the Torah and other sacred writings, the observation of Passover and additional biblical feasts connect Jews from every culture and generation. But of all the celebrations, Passover unifies them and tells their story best. Throughout the millennia, Passover has been a freedom cry for Israel, especially during their times of suffering. The Seder reminds the Jews of their identity as God's chosen people. "This year we are slaves; next year may we be free men." [7] It is the heart of their culture that points to God's deliverance and provision in Egypt and the desert.

Passover is technically the first night of a seven-day feast called The Feast of Unleavened Bread. The word "Seder" means order, and it's the process of observing the Passover ceremony and meal. Let's start at the very beginning.

God's Command To Remember
God instructed Israel to celebrate Passover as a lasting ordinance in Exodus 12:14, which they did during the Biblical period. Jewish history records that over time the rabbinical community discussed, debated and developed the Seder or "order" of the "telling," so that the people of Israel could observe it in unity, with all of its symbolic and historical meaning. The Haggadah - which means, "the telling" - is the book that contains

the established set of readings, prayers and blessings as well as explanations of the particular types of foods eaten during the meal. Globally, the Jewish community continues to observe Passover Seders today, some 3,300 years later.

For some evangelicals, reading liturgy or written prayers has a negative connotation. It can be perceived as archaic or spiritually lifeless. However, liturgy may surprise you! It can beautifully express the rich meaning of your faith - the words, insights and imagery that communicate deeper theological meanings. The story is told of an old Jewish rabbi who was approached by some young people from his synagogue. They told him: "We don't like the liturgy - it doesn't say what we are feeling." The old rabbi replied: "The purpose of the liturgy is not to express your feelings. The purpose of the liturgy is for you to repeat it until you have the feelings it expresses." Our hope is to show you the beauty of the Passover liturgy and the richness of this tradition. We encourage you to view the Seder as a sail that catches wind and moves you forward rather than an anchor that holds you back. Build on it and make it relevant to you, your friends and family.

The essence of the Seder is as follows: "You are to eat the meat, roasted in the fire, that night, along with bread made without yeast, and bitter herbs." (Exodus 12:8, NIV) The meat, the unleavened bread and bitter herbs are the foundational elements of the Seder. So, as long as you cover those three things, you've met the Old Testament requirements of the Seder.

Melanie:
I enjoy watching my son really get into playing
Pharaoh in our Seder skit and saying dramatically with
arms raised, "No! You may NOT take my slaves away."
to Moses. He's only five, so I'm not worried about him
playing the bad guy just yet.

Susie:
I loved watching little Israeli girls at a Seder act out the
Hebrew midwives by clutching baby dolls, squealing
and running away from the mean Pharaoh, played very
effectively by one of the dads! I'm not sure who
enjoyed it more, the children or their parents.

Any kind of creative activity you can fit into your Seder
will enhance its meaning and make it even more
enjoyable. Use your imagination (as well as online
tools like Pinterest) and make it your own. If children
are present – get them involved and engaged by
making it fun.

Getting Rid Of All Leaven

To prepare for Passover, most Jewish households
conduct a spring-cleaning of sorts. They diligently
search for and dispose of all leaven in the house. It is
after all, Passover and the Festival of Unleavened Bread
for Jews, so no leaven is allowed in the house for these
seven days. Leaven is used in scripture as a metaphor
for sin, so the cleansing of leaven from the home is
symbolic of cleansing ones heart from sin. In Jewish
households a common tradition is to have the children
search for the last bit of leaven (usually crumbs) placed
near a windowsill. A feather and a spoon are used to
gather the last of the leaven up, and then it's discarded

or burned in a fireplace or pit (see I Corinthians 5:6). As believers, we are to ask God to search our hearts, test us and show us any sin of which we need to repent (Psalm 139:23, 24). Spiritual preparation is an integral part of the Passover experience.

Seder Details

Passover begins at sunset during the full moon on the 14th day in the first month of the Jewish calendar called Nisan and lasts seven days. The eve of Passover is the appointed time for the Passover Seder. The Seder is significantly shorter on the other six nights, which is actually another feast, called The Feast of Unleavened Bread. We typically observe our Christian Passover on the Thursday before Good Friday and recommend you have your Seder a week or two prior to Easter – ideally during Holy Week.

The Seder is held in a home or large dining area and it is customary to invite guests. A typical Seder will include multiple families as well as friends and acquaintances. There is something extraordinary about participating in an event that is held globally by millions of people. The story, the questions, the responses and the spiritual conversations around the table all focus on the story of redemption, as well as the greatness and faithfulness of God. If you have children, include them. They play an important role in the Seder - after all, one of the key mandates in Passover is about teaching your children to carry on the tradition.

Adding the Christian perspective (explained in detail in Chapter 4) to the Passover readings shows God's plan of redemption through Jesus Christ, His Son.

You've most likely asked the question after experiencing Passover, "Why don't we, Christians, do this?" When Jesus instituted the New Covenant at Passover, He identified the wine as a symbol of His blood and the bread (matzah) as a symbol of His body that would be the substitutionary sacrifice for sin, just as the Passover Lamb was. This imagery would have been clearly understood by Jesus's disciples and early Jewish followers, as they were very familiar with the Passover story and Seder. However, when Jerusalem was destroyed and everyone was scattered across the Mediterranean, the gospel spread throughout the world. As it spread and the years went by, some believers (as early as the second century - 100 AD) observed Easter on the first night of Passover, focusing more on remembering Jesus's death as the sacrificial lamb; while others (Rome) celebrated Easter on the Sunday following Passover, emphasizing His Resurrection. At the Council of Nicaea in 325 AD, it was determined that Easter would focus on Jesus's Resurrection and be observed on the first Sunday after the full moon that directly followed the Vernal Equinox (March 21). Since communion (an abbreviated Passover) was observed more than once a year, it was decided Passover didn't need to be a yearly mandate. This is why the Christian Seder may be new to you. Passover morphed into the abbreviated Lord's Supper we are more familiar with - eating the bread and drinking the wine. This is how we've been taught to remember what Jesus did for us on the cross – in Communion. We aren't suggesting this is negative – this is just the backstory for those of you who like details!

Below is the Jewish Seder Order and elements of the Seder and how they tie to Christianity.

Typical Jewish Seder Order With Jewish Titles & Meaning[8]

Kaddesh	The First Cup of Wine
Ur'Chatz	The Washing of Hands
Karpas	Dipping the Vegetable
Yachatz	Breaking the Bread
Maggid	The Telling
Rachtzah	The Washing of Hands (a 2nd time)
Matzah	Eating the Matzah
Maror	Eating the Bitter Herbs
Korech	Eating the Hillel Sandwich
Shulchan Orech	Eating the Passover
Tzafun	Eating the Afikoman
Barech	Blessing After the Meal
Hallel	Offering Praise
Nirtzah	Conclusion of the Seder

Elements Of The Ceremonial Seder Meal

Unleavened Bread (Matzah): When Pharaoh released Israel from Egypt; they left immediately, with no time for their bread to rise. The sun beat down on the dough as they carried it along, and it baked into unleavened bread called Matzah. For Christians, the bread reminds us of Jesus, who was broken on our behalf.
The Green Vegetable (parsley, lettuce or celery): This symbolizes the growth and fertility of the Jewish people in Egypt, and springtime. For Christians it represents new life, growing and discipleship in Christ.
Salt Water: This recalls the sweat and tears shed by the Israelite slaves and also recalls Israel's journey crossing through the Red Sea from slavery to freedom. Believers in Christ are reminded that we crossed through the waters of Baptism to walk into freedom and eternal life.
Bitter Herbs (horseradish): This symbolizes and recalls the bitterness and harshness of slavery the Jews endured. We remember the bitterness of sin and our lives before Jesus.
Charoset (a mixture of apples, nuts, cinnamon and honey): This represents the mortar the Israelites were forced to make under Pharaoh's taskmasters. The sweetness also reminds them of the hope they had of freedom and to return to the Promised Land. It reminds us that our most difficult circumstances are sweetened by the hope we have in God.
Roasted Egg: This serves as a symbol of life and new beginnings. As Christians, it represents new life.
The Roasted Lamb Bone: It represents the first Passover Lamb, whose blood was put upon the doorposts of Israelites homes in Egypt. We are reminded of Jesus: "Behold the Lamb of God who takes away the sins of the world."

These foods eaten in the Seder are arranged on a "Seder Plate" or platter and placed on the table to be used during the ceremony (See image A).

Image A: Seder Plate with ceremonial foods.

The traditional Seder also adds four cups of wine or grape juice and is based upon the following verse: "I have heard the groaning of the Israelites… and I have remembered my covenant. Therefore, say to the Israelites: 'I am the Lord, and I will bring you out from under the yoke of the Egyptians. I will free you from being slaves to them, and I will redeem you with an outstretched arm… I will take you as my own people, and I will be your God" (Exodus 6:5-7, NIV).

The order of the Seder is built around the four cups.

The First Cup -- Cup of Sanctification: "I will bring you out." God separated Israel as His chosen people. As Christians, we are called out - to be separate from the world around us.
The Second Cup -- Cup of Deliverance: "I will free you." During this time in the ceremony, the focus is on the plagues and telling the story of Israel's deliverance (Exodus 12). We all have a story. Here, we remember and share the things He has done for us - He delivered us from the slavery and condemnation of sin.
The Third Cup -- Cup of Redemption: "I will redeem you to myself." The third cup reminds the children of Israel that they are His chosen, redeemed people by the blood of Lambs. This Cup of Redemption, taken after the meal, is when Jesus instituted the Lord's Supper, a sign of the New Covenant. It is at this point in the Seder we remember His blood shed and His body broken for us when we eat the Bread and drink the Wine.
The Fourth Cup -- Cup of Restoration: "I will take you as my people and I will be your God." This cup looks forward to the great feast, the Marriage Supper of the Lamb that we will one day share in Heaven with Jesus (Revelation 19:7-9). He did not drink from this fourth cup on that night. He is waiting to do that with us at the Marriage Supper of the Lamb in the Kingdom to come (Matt. 26:29).

The Four Questions

The four questions that help tell the story of deliverance begin with this question: "Why is this night different from all other nights?"[7] The adults around the table then tell the story of the Exodus and explain the reason they participate in this ritual each year. The Seder guide or Haggadah guides you through all these steps, so there is no memorization required.

The questions for children draw them into the celebration. If there are no children at your Seder, have the youngest of your guests read the four questions. The youngest child or person at the table begins "The Telling" of the story of the Exodus: "In the future, when your son asks you, 'What is the meaning of the stipulations, decrees and laws the Lord our God has commanded you?' tell him: 'We were slaves of Pharaoh in Egypt, but the Lord brought us out of Egypt with a mighty hand.'" (Deuteronomy 6:20-22, NIV).

After the youngest person at the table asks the question, the next person answers it and so on:

Why do we eat only unleavened bread on this night? Answer: When Pharaoh released our forefathers from Egypt they were forced to leave in a hurry. The sun beat down on the dough as they carried it, and baked it into unleavened bread called Matzah. For Christians, when we share in the bread of Passover and The Lord's Supper, we share in Christ who was broken on our behalf. He is the true Bread, the Bread of Life.
Why do we eat only bitter herbs on this night? Answer: We are reminded that our forefathers were slaves in Egypt and their lives were made bitter. Christians recall the bitterness of sin.
Why do we dip our vegetables in salt water? Answer: The parsley reminds us of the hyssop used to place the blood of the lamb upon the doorposts and lintels. The salt water reminds us of the Red Sea and of the tears shed while they were in bondage. The sweet charoset reminds us that our forefathers were able to withstand bitter slavery because it was sweetened by the hope of freedom. For us, even our most difficult circumstances are sweetened by our trust and hope in the Lord our God.
Why do we eat this meal in a reclining position? Answer: Reclining at the table was a sign of a free man in biblical times. Since our forefathers were freed on this night, we recline at the table, we are not eating in haste.

A typical Seder lasts about two hours. As the host of your group, you can skip around in your Seder guide if certain segments run long. If your group is having wine, the conversations could turn quite lively. During our research on this project, a family in Austin, TX who had just held their first Seder said, "It's no wonder the disciples fell asleep after drinking all that wine!" Note that in many Jewish Seders, they actually drink four entire cups of wine or juice. Our thinking is that it is best to just sip the wine/juice as the dinner progresses.

Interruptions are good in your Seder. It means people are listening and actively engaging. It is also a great opportunity for you to get a sense of where people are spiritually and how you might best respond. Prayer is key. Before you host your Seder, ask God to make your table a place where He is honored, the gospel is shared and where people feel comfortable asking questions and exploring the deeper aspects of their faith. Trust He will remind you of the things you need to remember.

Did You Know?
Animal sacrifices were part of Old Testament worship rituals during the first and second Temple eras (approximately 961 BCE – 70 AD). According to Jewish law, at Passover the lamb was to be slaughtered in Jerusalem at the Temple on Passover eve and then eaten with matzah and bitter herbs. However, in 70 AD the Romans destroyed not only Jerusalem, but the Temple as well. At that point, the practice of sacrificing a lamb was ended, but the rituals of the Passover Seder continued. The rabbis added the roasted egg to symbolize the sacrifice of the Passover lamb, as well as

the season of springtime and new life. It was also during this time that the festival transitioned into the home.[9]

The Passover Seder grew over time, with various versions reflecting the cultural influences on the Jews as well as different rabbinical streams of thought.[10] Today there are over 3,000 types of Haggadahs designed for specific religious sects, ethnic groups, age groups, you name it!

Chapter 4: Connecting the Dots - Passover, The Lord's Supper and The Marriage Supper of the Lamb

"What we call 'the Lord's Supper' is a foretaste of 'the Lamb's Supper' in Revelation 19. It's a beginning of the feast we eat with Jesus and his people in the new creation. It's not just a picture it's the real thing begun in a partial way." (Tim Chester, "A Meal with Jesus") [10]

As an observant Jew, Jesus would have celebrated the Passover feast all the years of His life (see Luke 2:41, John 2:13, 5:1, 6:4, 11:55-56). On the night before His crucifixion, Jesus ate His final Passover meal with His disciples. It was at that meal He instituted the New Covenant. The unleavened bread represented His sinless body and the wine, His blood. Historian Paul Maier puts it this way:
"In Old Testament worship, the flesh of a sacrificial animal was offered to God in order to obtain forgiveness. In the New Covenant, Jesus was Himself the paschal [Passover] lamb, sacrificed for our sin. This new covenant was clearly the fulfillment of the old, which began on Passover in Egypt. God was offering man a fresh contract or agreement in Jesus: His sacrifice on the cross would bring liberation, not from Egypt, but from the slavery of sin. The supper also foreshadowed the messianic banquet He would share with His followers in the future kingdom." [11]

When we examine the Passover Seder through a Christian lens, we see the entire story, the over-arching meta-narrative of God's plan of redemption for the world – from Passover to the Lord's Supper to the future Marriage Supper of the Lamb. Let's look at these a little more closely.

The Passover meal is the basis for the Lord's Supper (Communion or Eucharist), with the unleavened bread representing Christ's sinless body and the wine representing His blood.
In Luke 22:14-22 (also see Matthew 26:26 - 30; Mark 14:22-26) Jesus inaugurated what has been called "the longest continual meal in history."[12] The symbolic meaning of the bread and wine as His body and blood became an ordinance of the early church, along with baptism. (see Acts 6:1-7, 20:7-11) Communion is a historic practice of all Christian churches and denominations, in direct obedience to Jesus's command to "Do this in remembrance of Me."

It is not only a memorial meal but also a prophetic one. Theologian and author N.T. Wright puts it this way: "Jesus's central actions during the meal seem to have been designed to reinforce the point of the whole meal: the kingdom–agenda to which he had been obedient throughout his ministry was now at last reaching its ultimate destination. Passover looked back to the exodus, and on to the coming of the kingdom. Jesus intended this meal to symbolize the new exodus, the arrival of the kingdom through his own fate. The meal focused on Jesus' actions with the bread and the cup, told the Passover story and Jesus's own story and wove these two into one."[13]

Passover also looks to the future, the Marriage Supper of the Lamb, the vision seen by John in Revelation 19:7-10 (also alluded to in Isaiah 25:6-9, Matthew 22:1-14, 25:10, 26:29 and Luke 14: 15-24). This meal is celebrated in heaven as the ultimate banquet, for all those who are believers in Christ. It occurs after His bodily return, when He takes His own home with Him.

The idea of the Marriage Supper is clearer when we understand the wedding customs during Jesus's time (Second Temple). There were three distinct stages of the marriage ceremony. First, a contract would be made between the parents of the bride and bridegroom, including a dowry. This is what we call the "engagement," and is the stage Mary and Joseph were in when she became pregnant with Jesus. Secondly, after a period of months, the bridegroom would go to the house of the bride at midnight, with his friends. The bride would be ready to receive him, with her friends, and they would go with the groom to his home for the actual wedding. The third phase was the marriage supper and celebration, as described in John 2:1-2, the wedding in Cana, the site of Jesus's first miracle.

The Marriage Supper described in Revelation 19 implies that the first two "marriage" stages have already occurred. As it is generally understood, the first phase was completed on earth, when each Christian believed in Christ. The "dowry" paid was the blood of Christ, given for His bride, the church. Currently, the church (the bride) is in the second stage - engaged or betrothed to Christ and is waiting for Him to appear (see parable in Matthew 25:1-3). The third stage is the marriage supper, the banquet, celebrated in heaven at the end of time. This is the feast described in Revelation 19.

Some commentators believe that at the Last Supper Jesus did not drink the fourth cup, the Cup of Restoration. The third cup, the Cup of Redemption, was most likely when He established the New Covenant, with the bread and wine symbolizing His body and blood and the act of redemption. Luke puts this event "after the supper" (Luke 22:20), which is the third cup. Matthew, Mark and Luke all record Jesus's promise: that He would not partake of the Passover or the cup again until it found fulfillment in the Kingdom of God, meaning the future Messianic feast (see Matthew 26:27-29). We believe it is at this time, during this meal, that Jesus will drink the Cup of Restoration with His people in His kingdom. The Cup of Restoration represents the time when ALL things are restored and made new. "Then I saw a new heaven and a new earth, for the first earth had passed away" (Revelation 21:1-4, NIV). This fourth cup looks to the future, when all creation is restored to its original order, before it was marred by sin.

In the Christian Seder we see the ultimate story of God's plan of salvation for the world. All stories in Scripture fit into His redemption plan in some way. (For example, look at the story of Abraham and Isaac on Mount Moriah in Genesis 22:16-18). When you grasp the larger Biblical story, the redemption theme of the Bible becomes very clear: The Exodus Passover points to Jesus's Last Supper and New Covenant points to the Marriage Supper of the Lamb. We are living in the "in between" time in the present – between the Lord's

Supper and the Marriage Supper of the Lamb. Passover is an intersection of the past, the present and the future to come with each feast having the same theme: redemption, mercy and grace God has shown to His people.

Chapter 5: Should Christians Celebrate Passover?

It's important to note here that we are not suggesting that you MUST observe Passover. We are free from the law. Christians are not obligated or commanded to observe Passover, but there are convincing reasons to consider it.

Our intention is not to add more stress to busy family schedules. But some activities are worth the effort, and we believe this one certainly is. If it seems overwhelming, start small. Read Exodus 12 from your Bible or child's Bible as a family or group and enjoy a meal together. Adapt the "Seder for Kids" (located in the Appendix) to the age of your children and create your own family Passover tradition. We are introducing the Seder in its entirety to expose you to all aspects of this rich tradition, but we encourage everyone to make it their own. Start small and then add more steps year after year.

As we've shared Passover for Christians with churches and small groups, we've found that there are some who have added their own traditions that are especially meaningful to them. Miriam's Cup, Elijah's Cup, a crown of thorns, a nail - all these enhancements have helped make Passover more personal for families, communities, small groups and churches.

The evangelical world does not have specific traditions when it comes to Holy Week and Easter. Easter is actually the holiday we should own – not the Easter

Bunny. "For God so loved the world that He gave His only begotten Son, whoever believes in Him shall not perish but have everlasting life." The reason Jesus came – born of a virgin – was to die for our sins and be raised on the third day to redeem the world. Easter is the story of our redemption. Shouldn't we teach our children these truths? Couldn't we take a purposeful pause one night and share a meal with those we love, recounting the spiritual blessings we have received? Sharing the Passover meal from the Christian perspective is intentional time for believers to creatively present the biblical story of redemption fulfilled in Christ's death, resurrection and future return. Making this a part of your Holy Week or pre-Easter observances enables you to share the gospel, have spiritual conversations and explain Biblical truths while enjoying the camaraderie around the dinner table.

The Messianic community has celebrated Passover in this way for centuries. Why not expand that thought and practice to the Christian community?

If your guests are believers, the Lord's Supper can become part of this observance during the third cup (the cup of Redemption). If not, it's the perfect time to explain how Jesus instituted the Lord's Supper here, referring to Himself as the bread and the wine. He took our place. We do this to remember what He did for us. By the way, all this is detailed in the Christian Seder Guide located in the Appendix.

In John 17, after the Lord's Supper, Jesus prayed for us - that we may be "as one," even as God the Father, God the Son and God the Holy Spirit are one (John 17:11).

Passover is that one night every year, when all of Israel is unified, they are "as one." Globally, on that Passover Eve, Jews praise God and retell the story of their salvation and deliverance. Imagine Christians everywhere "as one" and in one accord blessing and praising God and honoring Jesus by telling His story around their tables. Using a "holy imagination," we can see God's smiling face as our prayers, praises and sincere hearts honor Him by remembering all He has done for us.

Melanie:
The first time Will and I hosted our Passover Seder; our sole objective was to honor Jesus in the Passover. As guests arrived, most of them had no clue about what we were about to do. They were curious, just like Will and I were the first time we participated in the Jewish Seder. As we read through the Christian Seder Guide it was like our guests – just like us years before – had found hidden treasures of truth within the pages of the Seder. "So this is how Passover links to the Lord's Supper?" "The Old Testament points to Jesus?" "Is that really true?" "Did God mean for that to happen?" My response, "Yes, let's talk about why…" Can you imagine these types of conversations happening around your table? Every year, Will and I invite a variety of guests to our Christian Seder; some are not Christians. We also intentionally invite at least one Jewish guest. This is a way for us to honor this Jewish tradition and have a conversation about how they celebrated it in the past with their families. One year my Jewish friend sang the four questions in Hebrew like she did years ago as a child. It was so beautiful hearing those ancient words sung. Passover is an experience. Imagine all your

guests around the table engaging, participating, praying, praising and remembering what Jesus did for you – together, "as one." This is an amazing thing. The bible says, when two or more are gathered in His name, He is there in our midst. He is there – we have felt His presence at our table.

Susie:
We have enjoyed going through the Kids' Seder at our Passover. We have six young grandkids and they ask me every year, "Are we going to do the Passover again?" The older ones read the scripture parts of the liturgy. The younger ones, who can't read yet, tell us the story of baby Moses, Miriam and Jochebed, and how God spoke to Moses from a burning bush. The Kids' Seder simplifies the ceremony and emphasizes their participation. They also have fun putting a drop of grape juice on their plates for each plague, naming them as they go. Of course, searching for the Afikomen always gets a little crazy. But looking at their little faces in the candlelight while going through the Seder is a gift that I will never take for granted. It's especially meaningful for my husband to put his hands on each one of them and pray for them at the conclusion of the meal.

Passover is a good time to remember the Jewish people and nation and pray for "the peace of Jerusalem." Pray that God will reveal Himself to your guests so they will see Him – Jesus, Yeshua - in the Passover. It is a wonderful tool to tell the gospel story and teach your children about the true heart of God. He loves them so much; He gave His life so that they may have life. So, should Christians celebrate Passover? We think, YES!

Did You Know?

Followers of Christ have been left a rich legacy of hospitality through stories found in the Old and New Testaments. The practice of sharing food and shelter with family and strangers alike was an integral part of the social fabric of life in Biblical times. Beginning with the Garden of Eden, God offered provision for Adam and Eve. They were given a choice of any food they so desired – that is, with one exception.

We see the generosity of a host opening his or her home to strangers through the stories of Abraham and his three angelic visitors, Rahab and the spies, and the women who provided accommodations for the prophets Elijah and Elisha, just to name a few. These stories illustrate the high value that culture placed on hospitality.

Jesus was frequently the recipient of this practice in the gospels, sharing meals with the disciples, with His dear friends (Lazarus, Mary and Martha), with curious seekers and even with His enemies. Scripture indicates He regularly observed the Passover, which was the most important observance on the first century Jewish calendar. It was at the table, and over a meal that some of His most powerful stories and teaching took place.

This practice became even more important in the first century early church. As the church was established and grew across the Mediterranean world, households were the location of church gatherings and served as a cohesive place for sharing news, the teaching of doctrine and fellowship (see Acts 2:46). The concept of hospitality was expanded to not just include one's extended family, but other believers in Christ, who were now a part of a larger family - the body of Christ.

Hospitality became more than just a cultural ritual but a holy duty and responsibility to the believing community (see 1 Peter 4:9 and Romans 12:13). Sharing meals together connects people on a level that nothing else can. When we intentionally provide food, conversation and an environment for social interaction, we are inviting others into our lives. There is no better or more effective way to share the story of Jesus and our own stories of how He has changed our lives than over a meal. Author and speaker Devi Titus says, "If home is where our hearts are formed, then the table is where our hearts are connected."[14]

When was the last time you ate together as a family at your dinner table? When was the last time you invited your neighbors over for a visit over a meal? The Seder is an intentional, creative and fresh way to demonstrate our love for one another. When we break bread together, when we drink the wine or juice together, we are to remember Jesus – God with us. Jesus did a lot of his ministry around the table over some bread and wine. You can do this – He will be with you.

Chapter 6: Experiencing Jesus in Passover

Melanie:

I was very excited as Will and I walked into Karen and Raoul's home to experience our first Passover Seder with Jewish Believers. There was a joyful spirit of belonging throughout the Seder. The traditional music was beautiful, and even featured professional singers. As they sang, it was like listening to angels singing in perfect harmony and rhythm. It reminded me of my younger days when my grandfather used to pull out his guitar and sing with my aunts and us grandkids at family gatherings – although we didn't sound nearly as good as they did. The plagues played an important role in their Seder, particularly for the children. The host placed water bottles intermittently along the table and the children put red food coloring in them to represent the Nile turning to blood. They reenacted the other plagues with the last one being death of the firstborn. At this time, we all placed red streamers over and around the door. "We are protected from death by the blood of the lamb," they said. The imagery was a wonderfully creative way to help us see and experience what happened all those years ago - and it was memorable for the kids.

When one of the children found the hidden Afikomen, the host had to pay a price to get it back. In this case it was what he had on hand – a $25 Amazon gift card. I don't think he was expecting to pay something. But, it's the rule – the Afikomen must be redeemed at a cost.

Note to the host; remember to have some candy or small bills on hand to redeem the Afikomen.

The Afikomen
Perhaps the most obvious picture of Christ in the Passover is seen in the afikomen. The picture of the coming Messiah is represented three ways in the afikomen. There is: 1) the imagery and meaning surrounding the broken bread, 2) the picture of the death, burial and resurrection of the "afikomen," and 3) the actual meaning of the Greek word "afikomen." These are explained in detail in Chapter 7 under "Breaking the Bread" and Chapter 9 under "Eating the Afikoman."

For our purposes in this chapter know that the Afikoman is the middle of three matzahs on the table. It was the Afikomen that Jesus held up and said, "This is my body, which is given for you; do this in remembrance of Me" (Luke 22:19). By identifying Himself as this bread, He is essentially saying, "I'm the One, I'm the Messiah!" Of all the ceremonial elements of the Seder meal, this is one of, if not the, most important.

The Cups
Who would have guessed the Passover Seder also illustrates how He would return? Consider this: Demonstrated within the Seder are two "comings" - Redemption and Restoration. These are explained in the third and fourth cups in the Seder. In the first "coming" (the third cup) the Messiah is the sacrificial Lamb who redeems the world. The next "coming" (the fourth cup) is the return of Christ, the conquering King

of Kings when there will be peace on earth and all things restored to its perfect state.

Covered By The Blood

Let's review the first coming of Jesus and how Passover reflects it in such a powerful way. Jesus is seen in the substitutionary sacrifice. When God gave Moses the Jewish law – the Torah, the first five books of the Bible – the Israelites were required to bring a sacrifice to the temple at the appointed times (including Passover). This sacrifice was the substitute given that covered the sins of the individual, family and even the entire nation of Israel. The sacrifices of the Old Testament were a temporary solution that pointed to the ultimate sacrifice that would be made once and for all (see Hebrews 10).

Passover also shows us how Christ's blood covers us and spares us from judgment. When Moses approached the court of Pharaoh with his brother, Aaron, asking for the release of the Israelites, Pharaoh refused. This meant that Egypt would have to endure nine terrible plagues with the final one being the death of the firstborn in each family. But unlike the previous plagues, the Israelites had to do something to avoid God's judgment. This scenario pointed to the ultimate sacrifice of the "Lamb of God" – Jesus. Passover and the blood of the innocent lamb is a powerful and intentional picture of redemption; it is the story of Israel's deliverance and is filled with Messianic imagery that Christians recognize as Jesus. When we trust in Jesus for our salvation, His blood is figuratively spread over our hearts, and we are spared from God's judgment.

The Lamb That Was Slain

God spoke of redemption with Abraham when He said, "Through your offspring all the nations on earth shall be blessed." (Genesis 26:4, NIV)

This picture of redemption becomes clear when we compare the Passover lamb traditions and Jesus's final week side-by-side.

Passover Tradition (Old Testament)	Jesus's Final Week (New Testament)
The Passover feast and sacrifice was to be held in Jerusalem. On the 10th day of the first month (Nisan 10), families were to select a lamb, a lamb without spot or blemish. (see Exodus 12:3-5, Deuteronomy 12:5, 16:5-6, 2 Samuel 24:18, 1 Chronicles 22:1, 6-10)	Jesus entered Jerusalem the Sunday (Palm Sunday) before Passover. It was the 10th day of the first month. (Matthew 21, Mark 11, John 12)

Passover Tradition (Old Testament)	Jesus's Final Week (New Testament)
The families were to care for the Lamb for four days and inspect it to make sure it was without defect. It had to be perfect. (see Exodus 12:5,6)	Jesus allowed Himself to be "inspected" at this time, teaching publicly in the Temple. He was tested and questioned by the religious leaders at this time. They were trying to trap Him. It was during that week the Pharisees began plotting His murder. (Matthew 21, John 12)
After those four days, on the 14th, they were to slaughter the lamb and roast it. They gathered their families and neighbors together to eat the meat along with bitter herbs and bread without yeast and tell the story of their deliverance to their children. (Exodus 12:3-8, 25-27)	That Thursday at sundown, Jesus celebrated His final Passover with His disciples. (Matthew 26, Mark 14, Luke 22, John 13)

Passover Tradition (Old Testament)	Jesus's Final Week (New Testament)
The priests inspected the lambs and declared them pure for the sacrifice.	After the Passover meal, late that night, Jesus was arrested and taken in the garden of Gethsemane. The Priests had him tried (falsely) and on Friday morning He was brought before Pilate. Pilate declared Him INNOCENT – PURE. Jesus had done NOTHING deserving of death. (Matthew 27:24, Mark 15:14, Luke 23:22, John 19:4)
On Friday, Priests sacrificed the lambs and gathered the blood in basins and sprinkled it on the altar. The lamb was roasted in the fire and not a bone broken. (Exodus 12:22)	On Good Friday, Jesus's was crucified. Blood flowed from His pierced hands, feet and side. He hung on the cross in the hot sun and not one of His bones was broken. (John 19:33)

Melanie:

In our Seder, after the meal and at the third cup, we shift into New Testament mode. The readings are clearly stated – Jesus is the bread that was broken. The wine represents his blood. We unashamedly share the gospel here. It's a solemn and special time when we remember what Jesus did for us, and all that entailed. It's here that we explain what we believe about grace and God's amazing love for us.

"Behold, the Lamb of God who takes away the sins of the world." (John 1:29, NIV) His blood shed for us. He took the punishment that we deserved. He did it. Jesus, the Passover Lamb who takes away the sins of the world has come and is coming again. "But He was pierced for our transgressions, he was crushed for our iniquities: the punishment that brought us peace was on Him, and by His wounds we are healed. We all like sheep, have gone astray, each of us has turned to our own way; and the Lord has laid on Him the iniquity of us all." (Isaiah 53:5-6, NIV)

We have been redeemed.

Did You Know?
One of the clearest pictures of redemption is found in Genesis 22. God required Abraham to sacrifice his only son, Isaac, as an offering. God miraculously sent a ram at the very last minute to be the burnt offering as a substitute, freeing Isaac from death. This wasn't some kind of accident, but an intentional event that pointed to the future Lamb of God. In her study "The Patriarchs," Beth Moore describes the events in detail, saying this was an "enactment." God was demonstrating a future event, when Christ would become our sacrifice by dying on the cross for our sins. Abraham pictured God, and Isaac pictured lost mankind. The ram, which was provided by God, was Jesus. God was showing Abraham and the world what

He was going to do. Beth Moore says: "The gospel was preached beforehand in the promise and portrayed beforehand on the mountain."[15] (See also Hebrews 11:17-19)

Jewish Believers describe Passover this same way. Passover is an "enactment" or performance showing Israel and the world His plan since the beginning of time. He commanded they observe the Passover every year forever so they would recognize Him when He came. God's desire is and has always been for us to be in communion with Him.

BOOK II: THE DETAILS OF PASSOVER – WHAT YOU NEED TO KNOW TO HOST A SEDER

Chapter 7: The First Cup, the Cup of Sanctification

These next chapters will walk you through the Seder and touch on the background, meanings and insights behind the prayers and order of the various blessings, traditions and readings from the Haggadah (the Seder Guide). If you are hosting a Seder, these chapters will help familiarize you with it. You will recall the order of the Seder stated in Chapter 3:

1. Kaddesh   The First Cup of Wine
2. Ur'Chatz   The Washing of Hands
3. Karpas   Dipping the Vegetable
4. Yachatz   Breaking the Bread
5. Maggid   The Telling
6. Rachtzah   The Washing of Hands
7. Matzah   Eating the Matzah
8. Maror   Eating the Bitter Herbs
9. Korech   Eating the Hillel Sandwich
10. Shulchan Orech Eating the Passover
11. Tzafun   Eating the Afikoman
12. Barech   Blessing After the Meal
13. Hallel   Offering Praise
14. Nirtzah   Conclusion of the Seder

1. Kaddesh: The First Cup of Wine: The hostess lights the candles and says the opening prayer: "Blessed are You, O Lord our God, King of the universe, Who has sanctified us by Your commandments and commanded us to kindle the festival lights." [16]

Jewish tradition says that a woman must light the candles and bless the lighting of them because the true Light of the World – the Messiah – would be born of a woman (Genesis 3:15). As Christians, we remember that Mary gave birth to Jesus, the Light of the World.

Once the candles are lit and blessed, it's time to bless the first cup of wine (or juice). "Blessed are You, O Lord our God, King of the Universe, Who creates the fruit of the vine." [16] The Creator of the Universe created the fruit of the vine and Jewish tradition holds that this is another reference to the Messiah. Jesus turned water into wine at His first miracle, which is another messianic connection with this First Cup. (John 2). Further, notice how the Jewish blessings bless God.

2. Ur'Chatz: The Washing of Hands: Next is the washing of the hands. All wash their hands at this time. You can use individual hand wipes, a basin with water or ceremonially "wash" by making hand-washing motions with your hands and napkin. Exodus 30:7-21 says Aaron and his sons were to wash their hands and feet at the bronze basin in the Tabernacle. This indicates internal reflection and agreement to obey God's laws with clean hands and pure hearts (Psalms 24:3-4).[17] This is possibly the time in the Seder when Jesus washed the feet of the disciples (John 13:4-17). As He did, He emphasized the importance of serving others with a sincere heart. We are encouraged to follow His example, by seeking to serve others.

3. Karpas: Dipping the Vegetable: At this point in the Seder the Seder plate is passed around and each person takes a sprig of parsley and dips it in the salt water

located on the Seder plate as well. Jewish tradition recalls their growth and fertility while in Egypt – God multiplied them and made them into a mighty nation. The salt water reminds them of the tears shed because of their terrible slavery and affliction.

4. Yachatz: Breaking the Bread: Next the host takes the three stacked matzah crackers located on a plate and covered with a napkin. He holds them up and takes the middle matzah out. He then sets the other two matzah down and breaks the middle matzah in half. The larger half he wraps in a cloth and sets it aside. This is the "afikomen" (pronounced ah-fee-KOH-muhn). If children are at the Seder, the host/or other adult, hides the afikomen for the children to find. If there are no children, just set it aside for later.

Some commentators believe the three Matzah represent Abraham, Isaac and Jacob. Others believe the three Matzah represent the people of Israel, the Priests and the Levites. But, all take the middle Matzot, break it and hide it. Whichever view you adhere to, both point to the Messiah. This middle matzah seen as "Isaac" reminds Israel of Abraham's test when Isaac was taken by his father to be sacrificed on Mount Moriah but was saved from death by God's provision. A ram – provided by God - caught in the bushes was offered up in Isaac's place. This is one of the clearest foreshadows in the Old Testament of the coming Christ, who would be provided by God as the substitutionary atonement for our sin. "For God so loved the world that He gave His only begotten Son, that whoever believes in Him should not perish but have everlasting life." (John 3:16, NIV)

The middle matzah seen as "the priest" reminds us that the Messiah, Jesus, is also our High Priest who provided eternal redemption once and for all in the Heavenly Holy of Holies. It is finished. "Therefore, holy brothers and sisters, who share in the heavenly calling, fix your thoughts on Jesus, whom we acknowledge as our apostle and high priest." (Hebrews 3:1, NIV) "But when Christ came as high priest of the good things that are now already here, he went through the greater and more perfect tabernacle that is not made with human hands, that is to say, is not a part of this creation. He did not enter by means of the blood of goats and calves; but he entered the most holy place once for all by his own blood, thus obtaining eternal redemption." (Hebrews 9:11-12, NIV) "Day after day every priest stands and performs his religious duties; again and again he offers the same sacrifices, which can never take away sins. But when this priest [Jesus] had offered for all time one sacrifice for sins, he sat down at the right hand of God," (Hebrews 10:11-12, NIV)

Messianic believers have another view: The three Matzah represent God the Father, God the Son and God the Holy Spirit. Notice the middle Matzah, the Son, Jesus, who was broken for us, buried and rose from the dead. All these views parallel with the practice of the Afikomen (broken, hidden and redeemed later after the meal.)

When Jesus took and broke the middle Matzah (that represented Him), he took the larger piece and wrapped it in a cloth then set it aside for later. This Afikomen is based upon the Greek word "aphikomenos" and has a few meanings: "he is coming," or "he has come" and "after the banquet" or "dessert."[18] Jewish tradition sees the Afikomen as meaning "dessert" and is eaten after the meal. Jewish believers and Christians see this as a clear reference to the Messiah. It means "he has come" and before He came, it meant, "he is coming" a direct reference to Christ.

Given the overall context and theological significance and imagery throughout the Passover Seder, it makes the most sense that the Afikomen is a reference to the Messiah – "He has come!"

Chapter 8: The Second Cup, the Cup of Deliverance

5. Maggid: The Telling: After the breaking the bread and setting the Afikomen aside, the host and all who are sitting around the table retell and recite the story of deliverance typically straight from Exodus Chapter 12 and sometimes other passages (see Chapter 2). The youngest person at the table asks the four questions (see Chapter 3). The other guests answer the questions, rotating, as directed in the Haggadah. Then, all drink the second cup of wine remembering His deliverance (See Chapter 3).

6. Rachtzah: The Washing of Hands (a second time): Before you eat the ceremonial foods and drink the second cup of wine, everyone washes their hands again. You will recall we washed our hands earlier in the Seder. Repeat it before the ceremonial meal is served on the Seder plate.

7. Matzah: Eating the Matzah: As everyone tells the story rotating turns around the table, the designated food on the Seder plate is eaten and explained. All eat the matzah (not the Afikomen) after the story is told. This is done to remember how unleavened bread was the bread eaten as the Hebrews left Egypt in haste. Let's look closely at this. Throughout the New Testament yeast is analogous with sin – a small amount of yeast affects a much larger amount of dough. The same holds true for our sin – even "small" sins can affect our entire character. The Matzah reminds us to reflect on our

lives and identify any sins that we need to address and ask forgiveness.

8. <u>Maror: Eating the Bitter Herbs</u>: Messianics believe that it was during the dipping of the bitter herbs that Jesus identified Judas as His betrayer. "While they were reclining at the table eating [the ceremonial foods and telling the story], he said, 'Truly, I tell you, one of you will betray me – one who is eating with me.' They were saddened, and one by one they said to him, 'Surely you don't mean me?' 'It is one of the twelve,' he replied, '<u>one who dips bread into the bowl with me.</u>'" (Mark 14:18-20, NIV)

9. <u>Korech: Eating the Hillel Sandwich</u>: In the days of the Second Temple, a disagreement arose among the priests and sages. The rabbi Hillel thought the matzah and bitter herbs should be eaten together; however, other rabbis thought they should be eaten separately. Therefore, the tradition developed into doing both ways – eat the bitter herbs separately first, then together with the Hillel Sandwich. The Hillel Sandwich is made by placing horseradish and charoset between two pieces of unleavened bread.

10. <u>Shulchan Orech: Eating the Passover Meal</u>: Once the ceremonial foods are eaten, everyone sets the Haggadahs aside and enjoy a festive meal. Tim Chester describes this type of meal, "The Lord's Supper should be a meal we 'earnestly desire' to eat. We should approach it with anticipation. With anticipation. With longing. With joy. The Lord's Supper should be a joyous occasion. A vibrant meal with friends. A feast."[19] A Passover Meal is similar to a Thanksgiving or

Christmas meal with everyone gathered, laughing, sharing and enjoying one another's company. This kind of meal shared among friends and families may be loud and messy but don't miss this – it is sacred!

Chapter 9: The Third Cup, the Cup of Redemption

11. <u>Tzafun: Eating the Afikoman</u>: After the meal, we pick up our Haggadahs and finish the Seder. It is time for the afikomen, the final item eaten. As mentioned before, this was the bigger broken half of the middle matzah, wrapped in a cloth and hidden or set aside. If there are children present, the Host, must redeem this piece of matzah at a price – usually a dollar or piece of candy. Think about this for a moment. This matzah was wrapped in a cloth (like a shroud); it was hidden away (buried) and then brought back at a cost (resurrected and redeemed). It's the image of the death, burial and resurrection of the Messiah told in the hiding and finding of the afikomen. This is done in Jewish households every year.

Remember what we've said before about the meaning of the word "afikomen?" "He is coming" or "He has come"? According to Luke's gospel, it was after the meal that Jesus took this bread, the afikomen. So, Jesus took this piece of "redeemed" matzah along with the third cup of wine, the cup of Redemption. This is when Jesus instituted Communion and introduced a New Covenant.

Let's examine closely what Jesus said at this time during their Seder. When He blessed the bread He gave the traditional Jewish blessing; "Blessed are you, LORD our God, King of the universe, who brings forth bread from the earth." [20]

This is the traditional blessing over the Afikomen at Passover. The statement "bread from the earth" takes on new meaning when we consider who this bread represents.

"During the meal, Jesus took and blessed the bread [with the blessing stated above], broke it and gave it to His disciples: Take, eat. This is my body." (Matthew 26:26, NIV) "This is my body" – He is identifying Himself as the Messiah – "He has come" - here in front of His disciples. He was also saying His body would be broken and then "brought forth" from the earth. Jesus foretells His resurrection a second time while blessing the this bread.[21]

Everything in the Seder points to Jesus, the Messiah. The afikomen clearly pictures Jesus, no matter how you look at it.

12. Barech: Blessing After the Meal: "Then He took a cup, and when He had given thanks, He gave it to them, saying 'Drink from it, all of you. This is my blood of the covenant, which is poured out for many for the forgiveness of sins. (Matthew 26:27-28, NIV)

This is the third cup, the cup of Redemption. Jesus establishes a New Covenant to be validated by His own blood. If you recall, the first covenant was made with Abram (Abraham before his name-change) in Genesis 15. There was another covenant made with Israel in the dessert when God gave the people the law (Exodus 24). The blood used to confirm that Old Covenant was temporary. These sacrifices looked forward to the ultimate, perfect sacrifice and redeemer

– they were a foreshadowing of the Messiah to come. (Colossians 2:17)

"'The days are coming,' declares the Lord, 'when I will make a new covenant with the people of Israel and with the people of Judah. It will not be like the covenant I made with their ancestors…' 'This is the covenant I will make with the people of Israel after that time,' declares the Lord, 'I will put my law in their minds and write it on their hearts. I will be their God, and they will be my people. No longer will they teach their neighbor, or say to one another, 'Know the Lord, 'because they will all know me, from the least of them to the greatest,' declares the Lord. 'For I will forgive their wickedness and will remember their sins no more.'" (Jeremiah 31:31-34, NIV)

It is at this time during the Cup of Redemption that Jesus announced the New Covenant. Many Jewish believers compare this with marriage customs during first century Judaism. In ancient times when a marriage contract was being negotiated, there was a bride price to be paid. After that was agreed on, then all would share a cup of wine to seal and confirm the pledge. The traditional blessing of the wine: "Blessed are you, O Lord our God, King of the universe, creator of the fruit of the vine." That night Jesus explains that He is the vine and we are the branches that are called to bear fruit. "I am the vine; you are the branches. Whoever abides in me and I in him, he will bear much fruit, for apart from me you can do nothing." (John 15:5, NIV) Creator of the fruit of the vine.

In the book, "A Meal with Jesus," Tim Chester says, "The Lord's Supper is a call to God to act in keeping with his covenant: forgiving us, accepting us, and welcoming us to the Table through the finished work of Christ."[22]

It is finished with Jesus. He completed His mission. When we drink the cup of Redemption and eat the Afikomen – this is where we recognize Jesus as Messiah and agree that He is our Savior. He did what no human being could ever do – live a sinless life, give His life on the cross and raise it again three days later. "For God so loved the world that He gave His one and only Son, that whoever believes in Him shall not perish but have eternal life." (John 3:16, NIV)

Chapter 10: The Fourth Cup, the Cup of Restoration

13. Hallel: Offering Praise: After the Afikomen is eaten and the third cup of wine drunk, it is now time for the fourth cup, The Cup of Restoration. This is referred to as the cup of praise because Psalms 118 and 136 are recited and we are reaching the end of the (sometimes very long) Seder.

Jesus did not drink this cup, according to scripture. "For I tell you I will not drink again from the fruit of the vine until the kingdom of God comes." (Luke 22:18,NIV) This is why we prefer to call this cup the cup of Restoration. What we call 'the Lord's Supper' is a foretaste of 'the Lamb's Supper' in Revelation 19. It's a beginning of the feast we eat with Jesus and His people in the new creation.

Passover is an intersection of the past, present and future to come. The past – Israel is saved from Egypt and walks boldly and miraculously into the Promised Land. The present – Jesus, the Lamb of God brings salvation to the world and establishes the New Covenant. The future – Jesus IS coming again as the conquering King of Kings to restore the world to Himself.
At the end of the Seder all say joyfully, "Next year in Jerusalem!" [23] At the end of time, God will reveal the new heaven and new earth, where we will celebrate the Marriage Supper of the Lamb in the New Jerusalem.

"Then I saw 'a new heaven and a new earth,' for the first heaven and the first earth had passed away, and there was no longer any sea. I saw the Holy City, the New Jerusalem coming down out of Heaven from God, prepared as a bride beautifully dressed for her husband. And I heard a loud voice from the throne saying, 'Look! God's dwelling place is now among the people and God himself will be with them and be their God. 'He will wipe every tear from their eyes. There will be no more death or mourning or crying or pain, for the old order of things has passed away." (Revelation 21:1-4, NIV)

We live in a broken and sinful world, which wasn't God's original design. But one day all things will be as they should be – restored to His original purposes. In His kingdom there will be no more sorrow and no more tears. At that Feast of all Feasts we will all drink that fourth cup together.

Concluding their Passover meal, Jesus and His disciples sang a song (the "hallel") and made their way to the Mount of Olives. (Matthew 26:3)

14. Nirtzah: Conclusion of the Seder: "Next Year in Jerusalem!" [23] The Passover Seder is complete. The host says a final blessing, the blessing given by God to Aaron and Israel (Numbers 6:24-26, NIV): "The Lord bless you and keep you, The Lord make his face shine upon you and be gracious to you, The Lord turn his face toward you and give you peace! Amen!"

While we've added New Testament thinking to this Jewish Seder and tradition, the Jewish people have been doing this for about 3,300 years, since the time of Moses. Can you see Jesus IN this? Passover is about Jesus.

Chapter 11: Ok, How Do I Do A Seder?

Many of our Jewish friends say that some of their best memories are from past years at their family's Passover Seder. A typical Passover gathering may go something like this: Family or close friends arrive about two hours before the Seder begins to help out. They bring covered dishes like mashed potatoes, roasted vegetables and various kugels (a baked casserole Jewish dish). These dishes are added to the meals already prepared and laid out on the kitchen counter or table. Then the assignments begin – someone to man the matzah ball soup, kids to crack and chop nuts for the charoset, someone to grate the maror (horseradish root) and someone else to chop the apples. The Seder Table would be set and ready to receive more family, neighbors and friends who would soon arrive. At times chaotic, at other times quiet and reflective, the family Seder creates memories that last a lifetime.

A common joke among families is that for kids, and some adults, a Passover Seder can sometimes feel longer than the 40 years their ancestors spent in the desert! Therefore, it's important to make it a meaningful experience for all, without sacrificing the purpose and fun. If there are children at the Seder table, you will want to have things ready for them to keep them engaged and interested.

Setting Your Table For The Seder

Ceremonial Foods:	
*Boiled or Roasted Egg	*Charoset (apple, nut, honey mixture)
*Lettuce or Parsley	*Horseradish
*Salt Water	*Roasted Lamb Bone
Wine or Grape Juice	Matzah

   *These ceremonial foods are placed on the Seder Plate or Platter.

Ceremonial Items:
Candles
Seder Plate or Platter
Matzah Cover or Napkins to cover Matzah
Haggadah/Seder Guides for each place setting

Image B: Table Set For the Seder

Keep the menu simple. Don't stress out. Your guests will enjoy your home and hospitality as they share a special meal with you and everyone at the table. Shauna Neiquest, in her book "Bread & Wine" encourages families to move meals back to the table, with face-to-face conversations. She advises those who aren't accustomed to having people in their home to start where they are. "If you don't cook, begin by inviting people over. Order pizza and serve it with a green salad and a bottled salad dressing. Get comfortable with people in your home, with the mess and chaos."[24] If you focus on making people comfortable and happy, it will be a success. It's not about the food – it's about the people. Welcome them and they will feel special.

Typical Passover Menu

Matzah Ball Soup
Green Salad
Chicken, Brisket, Salmon or Lamb
Spinach or Dark Green Vegetable
Potato or Rice Dish
Ratatouille (eggplant, zucchini casserole)

Melanie:
Will and I usually roast a lamb and make matzah ball soup. We invite our guests to bring other foods that may have been common back in Moses's day. With so many kosher recipes available online and on Pinterest, it's easy to find something unique and fun to make. Remember, as Christians we are not bound by Jewish dietary rules or customs. So your meal doesn't have to be kosher. Start where you are. If you make a great lasagna or enchilada dish – do that. If you have time constraints, you can always pick something up at your local grocery or deli.

Susie:
My style differs from Melanie's. I usually pick up something my entire family can enjoy – including the grandkids - like Italian take out! The key idea is to spend time together focused on the true meaning of Easter – Jesus became our Passover Lamb.

Image C: Lighting the candles at the Passover Table

We've spoken to many groups about Passover these past few years and know this can seem intimidating. Let's address the key concerns you might have.

One we hear frequently is: "I'm single and don't have a family." Remember, Jesus was single and He celebrated this feast!

Melanie: I was 33 when Will and I married. Until then, I was always looking for a reason to have a party. I'm that person who loved having all my friends over for football watching parties, Mad Men Parties, etc. How about a Passover Party? Yes, indeed! If you think about it, it could be a great way to meet Mr. Right!

So much of Jesus's teaching was around a dinner table. In the book, "A Meal With Jesus," Tim Chester writes, "Jesus spent his time eating and drinking – a lot of his time… His mission strategy was a long meal, stretching into the evening. He did evangelism and discipleship around a table with some grilled fish, a loaf of bread and a pitcher of wine."[25] Evangelism Explosion. The Roman Road. All of those methods are excellent tools. But remember, developing relationships with others over a meal can also be a very effective way of sharing the gospel. Passover is about sharing YOUR spiritual story with others, just like Jesus did. You don't have to be married to do that.

Another concern we hear is: "I don't have kids." You don't have to have children to have a Seder – again, think about Jesus. It's talking, teaching, sharing and connecting with others, so gather your friends and family together and just do it!

And finally, a big one we hear is: "I'm just too busy. I work fulltime and have to get my kids to baseball practice, they've got homework, and I've got family obligations, and a hundred other things. My plate is full." There is no question that everyone's lives are jam packed with activities. You have to create a space for this.

Melanie: When Will and I became parents, our priorities changed significantly. We saw Passover as something we could do as a family to teach Nicholas our spiritual values. It's become our tradition and our desire is that Nicholas would do the same when he has his own family. I imagine someday being invited to his Seder at Easter and seeing him lead his own family in Passover - what a legacy!

Keep in mind that you can host your Passover any time before Easter – not just the Thursday night before Good Friday. Our Seder is sometimes held two weeks ahead of time, due to family schedules. However, the closer it is to Holy Week, the better.

I'll never forget driving home with Will after our first Seder. It was all about Jesus, even though He wasn't mentioned once. The thought that kept coming back to us was: "Why don't Christians do this? Why don't I know about this?" It was a life changing experience – it enhanced our faith.

When we remember God's faithfulness in the past, it makes it easier for us to believe and trust He will keep His promises in the future. Jesus came and is coming again. We must teach others and tell His story. You CAN do this. And when you do, your Easter will NEVER be the same.

Chapter 12: What's Your Story?

One of the key customs at Passover is to relate personally to the story as though you, yourself came up out of Egypt. As Christians, we understand another perspective – we were slaves to our sins and in Jesus we are set FREE!

John 14:26, NIV says: "But the Advocate, the Holy Spirit, whom the Father will send in my name, will teach you all things and will remind you of everything I have said to you." The Holy Spirit teaches and reminds us of the things we need to know and say. Remember when God commanded the people of Israel to keep the Passover as an ordinance forever? It was to pass on the stories to the following generations. What a wonderful opportunity to start a new tradition of telling your own story during Holy Week and the Easter season. Sharing with our friends, family and neighbors what God has done for us is a privilege and responsibility. Your friends have stories too – maybe experiences they haven't thought about in years. Know that the Holy Spirit will guide those conversations – God will be glorified around your table and you will be blessed!

Throughout the course of the meal, your guests will ask you questions about the Seder. Our prayer is that God will give you the words to say when that moment comes. But to prep, let's do a little pre-work. You may not have thought about your story in ages. Prayerfully work through this exercise. We pray the Holy Spirit will bring those relevant memories to mind as you work through two or three or all of these questions.

What's your spiritual journey? It can start anywhere –
from your birth or your Christian birth. Grab a
notebook or journal and write it out. Stick to the major
events, the significant markers in your life. Here are
some questions to help spark your stories: It may be
easier to think about your life chronologically - by
elementary years, high school years, college, etc. What
was your home like spiritually? Is there a spiritual
heritage from your family? If not, think about that – are
you the first to begin a spiritual legacy?

Who has had the greatest impact on your life
spiritually? Were you involved in church or Christian
education growing up? If so, how did this impact you?
Were there any major events that happened to you?
How did this impact and influence your life? If you are
a believer, write out your testimony highlighting the
moment you decided to follow Jesus. What did that
mean to you at the time? How has your Christian walk
changed over the years? Has anything happened this
year that God had a hand in?

It's good to know your story so you are ready to share
when the appropriate time comes. The first time you do
it may be clunky, but with practice, it will flow
smoothly. Our primary purpose in this chapter is for
you to look at your life highlighting significant spiritual
events that glorify and honor God. What are those
milestones that have occurred and brought you to the
place you are now?

Knowing your own story and telling it often will help
you lead and host a meaningful and engaging Seder.

You can share parts that fit in nicely with the Seder flow – Sanctification, Deliverance, Redemption and Restoration. You will find that when you share, others will feel safe and comfortable to do the same.

Now, it's your turn. Send out invitations (we use Evite) to your friends, family and neighbors and Host your first Christian Passover Seder. By celebrating Passover you are starting a unique legacy for your family. Join us and let's start a Movement. A Movement that involves millions of worshipers with ONE voice remembering what God has done, what God is doing and what God will do in our lives!

BOOK III: TOOLS YOU NEED TO HOST YOUR OWN PASSOVER SEDER

Seder Guide: Complete

<u>INSTRUCTIONS on How To Use This Seder Guide</u>:
This Seder Guide should be used as a tool to help inspire as well as enhance your Seder experience. By focusing and learning about Passover we see how Jesus fulfills this ancient celebrated feast.

As you gather your group together to participate in this Passover Feast be sure everyone has a copy of this guide. You will read through this document rotating from person to person. Instructions are written throughout feel free to read aloud or not as you go along.

Designate a host and hostess for your group, as each have specific tasks and help lead and guide the Seder. Keep in mind, Passover is, by tradition, an inclusive holiday and all are invited to participate – you don't have to know what to do or what comes next because the guide will walk you through it!

If you and your group prefer to say your own prayers instead of the written prayers, feel free to do so.

LIGHTING OF THE CANDLES

The Hostess lights the candles to begin the Seder.
While lighting the candles prays:

HOSTESS:
Blessed are You, O Lord our God, King of the universe,
Who has sanctified us by Your commandments
And commanded us to kindle the festival lights.

Blessed are You, O Lord our God, King of the universe,
Who sanctified us with His commandments,
And commanded us to be a light to the nations
And Who gave to us Jesus our Messiah the Light of the world.
May our home be consecrated, O God,
By the Light of Your countenance,
Shining upon us in blessing and bringing us peace.

ALL: AMEN

If you prefer to say your own prayer here, that's ok. The primary purpose here is to initiate the lighting of the candles, recognizing Jesus as the Light of the world, kicking off your Passover Seder and blessing your time together.

On a large serving plate are the elements of the Seder - a dish of salt-water, horseradish, green herb (e.g. parsley), a bone from the lamb and haroset (apple, honey nut mixture). The wine and matzah are set near the Host.

[Host or Hostess explains the elements of the Seder &

Seder Plate.]

HOST/HOSTESS: Let us review the items on the Seder Plate.

Unleavened bread, Matzah: called "bread of affliction" because it recalls the unleavened bread prepared for the hasty flight by night from Egypt. The bread is broken during the Seder reminding us of Jesus's words, "this is my body."

A Green Vegetable, such as parsley: symbolizes the growth and fertility of the Jewish people in Egypt. For Christians it represents our new life and growing in our faith.

Salt Water: recalls the sweat and tears shed by the Israelite slaves and also recalls the splitting of the Red Sea as Israel passed from slavery to freedom. As Christians, we are reminded that we crossed through the waters of baptism to walk into freedom and eternal life in Jesus.

Bitter Herbs, the horseradish: Recalls the bitterness and harshness of slavery the Jews endured. As Christians, we recall the bitterness of the slavery of sin.

The Haroset, a mixture of apples, nuts, and honey: Represents the mortar the Israelites were forced to make under Pharaoh's taskmasters. The sweetness reminds them of the hope they had in freedom. For us, it reminds us that even in the toughest circumstances they are sweetened by our hope in God.

The Roasted Lamb Bone: A reminder of the Temple Sacrifice and the first Passover Lamb whose blood was put upon the doorposts of Israelites homes in Egypt. Jesus was our Passover Lamb who takes away the sins of the world once and for all.

A Roasted Egg: Serves as a symbol of life and new beginnings. As Christians, we know it's never too late for a new beginning!

THE BLESSING OF THE FEAST

HOST'S PRAYER:
Blessed are You, O Lord our God, King of the Universe,
Who has chosen us above all peoples,
And has exalted us above all tongues,
And has hallowed us with Your commandments.
In love, You have given us, O Lord our God,
Seasons for gladness, holy-days, and times for rejoicing.

This day of the feast of the unleavened bread,
The time of our freedom, an assembly day of holiness,
Is a memorial to the Exodus from Egypt. Today we also remember what Jesus did for us on the cross. He redeemed us from the slavery of sin.

You have chosen us and have sanctified us above all peoples,
And You have given us Your sacred seasons for our inheritance.
Blessed are You, O Lord, Who sanctifies Israel,
Brothers and Sisters in Christ and the festivals.

MIRIAM'S CUP (OPTIONAL)

(Optional: You May Choose to Skip this Page and Go To THE WASHING OF HANDS Section)

ALL ROTATE EACH PARAGRAPH:
Some Passover celebrations include a special cup called "Miriam's Cup" to honor the role of women in Jewish households and history. It is placed beside the Cup of Elijah. This is the cup of Miriam, the cup of living waters, a reminder of how God provided water in the desert during our Exodus from Egypt.

Miriam's cup is currently empty, I invite the women of at our Seder table to fill Miriam's cup with water from their own glasses.
Pass Miriam's cup around and WOMEN fill it with water from their water glass. While the cup is being passed around the table, continue to read.

Jewish Tradition teaches that a miraculous "well" accompanied the Hebrews throughout their journey in the desert, providing them with water. This well was given by God to Miriam, to honor her bravery and devotion to the Jewish people. Miriam and her well were a spiritual oases in the desert, sources of sustenance and healing. Her words of comfort gave Hebrews faith and confidence to overcome the hardships of the Exodus.

We fill Miriam's cup with water to honor her role in ensuring the survival of the Jewish people. As keepers of traditions in the home, women passed down songs and stories, rituals and recipes, from mother to daughter, from generation to generation. As we fill the cup of Miriam with water from our own glasses, our prayer is that our daughters may continue to draw from the strength and wisdom of our heritage.

Paul mentions a "spiritual rock" that followed the Israelites in the dessert and provided water to them. He associated this "Rock" with Jesus, who is the Living Water. "For I do not want you to be ignorant of the fact, brothers and sisters, that our ancestors were all under the cloud and that they all passed through the sea. They were all baptized into Moses in the cloud and in the sea. They all ate the same spiritual food and drank the same spiritual drink; for they drank from the spiritual rock that accompanied them, and that Rock was Christ." *(I Corinthians 10:1-5)*

For Discussion (Optional): Would anyone like to share a story of a strong woman in your family and the impact she had on you? This can be a spiritual impact or a story that honors your heritage. All can participate in this.

THE WASHING OF HANDS – Place wet naps near each place setting for the "washing" of hands. You may recall in the Last Supper when Jesus washed the feet of the disciples, it was probably at this point that He did that. Read this verse while "washing" hands.

ALL "WASH" HANDS

PERSON TO THE LEFT OF THE HOSTESS READS,
ROTATE EVERY PARAGRAPH:
"After that, he poured water into a basin and began to
wash his disciples' feet, drying them with the towel that
was wrapped around him... When he had finished
washing their feet, he put on his clothes and returned
to his place. "Do you understand what I have done for
you?" he asked them. "You call me 'Teacher' and
'Lord,' and rightly so, for that is what I am. Now that I,
your Lord and Teacher, have washed your feet, you
also should wash one another's feet. I have set you an
example that you should do as I have done for you."
(John 13:5, 12-15)

NEXT PERSON READS:
REVIEW THE SPECIAL ORDER OF THE SEDER –
During the Seder we drink 4 cups of wine. These cups
have spiritual significance. The Seder is divided into 4
parts according to the 4 cups of wine. We drink the first
two cups before the Passover Meal is served. Then the
Passover meal is served and eaten. Then after the meal,
two more cups are consumed to complete the Passover
Seder.

The four cups represent the promises God made to the
children of Israel while they were still in Egypt.

Exodus 6:5-7: "Moreover, I have heard the groaning of
the Israelites, whom the Egyptians are enslaving, and I
have remembered my covenant. Therefore, say to the
Israelites: 'I am the Lord, and I will bring you out from
under the yoke of the Egyptians. I will free you from
being slaves to them, and I will redeem you with an
outstretched arm and with mighty acts of judgment. I

will take you as my own people, and I will be your God. Then you will know that I am the Lord your God, who brought you out from under the yoke of the Egyptians."

The 4 Cups represent the following:
Cup of Sanctification: "I will bring you out." Readings are focused on God separating Israel as His chosen people. As Christians, we are called out – to be separate from the world around us.

Cup of Deliverance: "I will free you." During this time in the ceremony the focus is on the plagues and telling the story of Israel's deliverance. We all have a story too.

We remember and share the things He has done for us – He delivered us from the slavery of sin. After this second cup and readings, we will break for the Passover meal.

Cup of Redemption: "I will redeem you to myself". After the meal is finished, the third cup reminds the children of Israel that they are His chosen, redeemed people by the blood of lambs. This Cup of Redemption is where Jesus instituted the Lord's Supper. Here He instituted a new covenant. It was at this point in the Seder we are to remember His blood shed and His body broken for us when we drink the Wine and eat the Bread. He Redeemed us. In the Old Testament Passover He saved His People, Israel. In the Lord's Supper Jesus redeems the World once and for all in a New Covenant.

Cup of Restoration: "I will take you as my people and I will be your God." This cup looks forward to the great feast we will one day share in Heaven with Jesus. He didn't drink from this 4th cup that night. He's waiting to do that with us at the Marriage Supper of the Lamb.

As Christians we are called out to be separate from the world around us. Jesus delivered us from the slavery of sin when He redeemed us by dying on the cross. We now look forward to His return as King of Kings and Lord of Lords when He will take us as His own and He will be our God and we will dwell with Him forever.

THE CUP OF SANCTIFICATION – *Pour the first glass of wine.* "I will bring you out."

ALL:
Blessed are You, O Lord our God, King of the Universe, Who creates the fruit of the vine.

After this blessing, all drink the first cup.

BLESS THE CHILDREN: If children are present, this is the time parents place their hands on each of their children's heads and bless them. Again, feel free to say your own prayer over your children. If no children present, skip to "Dip the Vegetable."

Lord, let your salvation spring up within (CHILD'S NAME), that (he/she) may obtain the salvation that is in Christ Jesus, with eternal glory. (Isaiah 45:8, 2 Timothy 2:10)
Heavenly Father, May integrity and honesty be (CHILD'S NAME) virtue and protection. (Psalm 25:21)

DIP THE VEGETABLE: The Seder Plate is passed to all so everyone can take a piece of parsley. All dip the parsley in the salt water.
The parsley (or green vegetable) symbolizes the growth and fertility of the Jewish people in Egypt. It also recalls their great suffering. We eat parsley dipped in salt water to remember the tears shed during the time of oppression and slavery in Egypt. For Christians, it represents new life, growing in His word and discipleship in Jesus.

All take the parsley, dip it in the salt-water, and say:
Blessed are You, O Lord our God, King of the Universe, Who creates the fruit of the soil.

All eat the parsley.

THE MATZAH: The host lifts the 3 Matzahs, then takes the Middle Matzah and breaks it in two. He places the larger piece back with the others (still in the middle) and wraps the smaller piece in a cloth that is hidden for the children to find. If there are no children, just set this off to the side for later use.

The Middle Matzah that is removed is called the Afikomen. We will discuss this more following the meal.

HOST: This is the bread of our affliction our fathers ate in the land of Egypt. Let all who are hungry come and eat. Let all who are in want come and celebrate the Passover with us. May it be God's will to redeem us from all evil and from all slavery.

As Believers in Christ, we too celebrate this Seder. Jesus celebrated Passover all the years of His life including the night before he died. As we participate in this Seder, consider your salvation and how the Lord, rescued you, personally, from the slavery of sin into eternal life and freedom in Jesus Christ.

THE 4 QUESTIONS:
"On that day tell our son, 'I do this because of what the LORD did for me when I came out of Egypt.'" *Exodus 13:8*

The youngest child/person at the table asks the questions below.
"Why is this night different from all other nights?

On all other nights we eat either leavened or unleavened bread, but on this night why only unleavened bread?

On all other nights we eat vegetables and herbs of all kinds; why on this night do we eat only bitter herbs?

On all other nights we never think of dipping herbs in water or in anything else; why on this night do we dip the parsley in salt water and the bitter herbs in haroset?

On all other nights we eat either sitting upright or reclining; why on this night do we recline as we partake of the four cups of wine?

Answering the Questions (All rotate answering the Questions): "I'm glad you've asked these questions.

Exodus 12:26-27: And when your children ask you, 'What does this ceremony mean to you?' then tell them, 'It is the Passover sacrifice to the Lord, who passed over the houses of the Israelites in Egypt and spared our homes when he struck down the Egyptians.'" Then the people bowed down and worshiped.

Why do we eat only matzah? When Pharaoh released our forefathers from Egypt they were forced to leave in great haste. They had little time to bake their bread and could not wait for it to rise. The sun beat down on the dough as they carried it along, and baked it into unleavened bread called Matzah. For Christians when we share in the bread of Passover and The Lord's Supper, we share in Christ who was broken on our behalf. He is the true Bread, the Bread of Life.

Why do we eat bitter herbs? So that we are reminded that our forefathers were slaves in Egypt and their lives were made very bitter. We remember the bitterness of sin and our lives before Jesus.

Why do we dip the herbs tonight? The parsley reminds us of the hyssop used to place the blood of the lamb upon the doorposts and lintels. The salt water reminds us of the Red Sea and of the tears shed while they were in bondage. The sweet haroset reminds us that our forefathers were able to withstand bitter slavery because it was sweetened by the hope of freedom. For us, it reminds us that even in the toughest circumstances they are sweetened knowing we can trust and hope in the Lord our God.

Why do we recline at the table? It is because reclining was a sign of a free man long ago, and since our forefathers were freed on this night, we recline at the table. Jesus said, "Come to me, all you who are weary and burdened, and I will give you rest." Matthew 11:28

NEXT PERSON *(All rotate)*
"And you shall observe this event as an ordinance for you and your children forever." *(Exodus 12:24)*

"And when your children say to you, 'Why are we doing this?' tell them: 'It's the Passover-sacrifice to God who passed over the homes of the Israelites in Egypt when he hit Egypt with death but rescued us.'" *(Exodus 12:26-27)*

For Discussion (Optional): While Israel was in Egypt they became a great nation. They remained separated from Egypt. How has God called you to be separate from the world around you?

THE CUP OF DELIVERANCE, *The Second Cup is poured*: "I will rescue you."

All raise the second cup.
So, this promise, "I will rescue you," made to our forefathers holds true also for us. For more than once the enemy risen up to destroy Israel and Christians. But the Lord our God, Saves us!

Put the cup down.

The Plagues: Here, the plagues are recited. All dip their finger in the second cup of wine or juice and recite each of the plagues while dotting the edge of each plate.

These were the ten plagues that God brought upon the Egyptians in Egypt.

Dip your finger in the wine and dot the edge of your plate while reciting the plagues.

ALL: Blood, Frogs, Gnats, Flies, Sickness, Boils, Hail, Locusts, Darkness, Death of the Firstborn. *(Your plate should have dots of wine/juice along the edge)*.

We do this because our joy is diminished due to the suffering of the Egyptian people. God has taught us to love our enemies and not to rejoice when our enemy falls. God's love is for everyone, therefore, our second cup isn't completely full because our joy is not complete.

NEXT PERSON:
Now, it is our duty from year to year to tell the story of Israel's deliverance from Egypt. The sages tell us that to dwell on it at length is accounted as praiseworthy.

We can also rejoice and keep the Passover as Christians. It reminds us of our own need for salvation. We were once slaves to sin and The Lord rescued us with a mighty hand and outstretched arm.

THE TELLING: The Story of Israel's Deliverance
(All rotate reading each paragraph)

Summarized from Genesis 47:4; Deuteronomy 10, 26; Exodus 1, 2

This is how we came to Egypt. My father and his family went down to Egypt, and lived there. We were few in number when we went, only 70 people. We moved from Canaan because there was a great famine and we needed food and pasture for our flocks. Joseph arranged with Pharaoh for us to sojourn in the land of Goshen. While we were there we became a great nation.

We multiplied and became like the stars of heaven. We grew strong, great and powerful, and the Egyptians became afraid. They afflicted us and laid upon us hard bondage. We cried out to the Lord, the God of our fathers, and the Lord heard our voice, saw our affliction, toil and oppression, and God remembered His covenant with Abraham, Isaac and Jacob and the Lord brought us out of Egypt with a mighty hand and outstretched arm and with great dread, and with signs, and with wonders.

Exodus 12:1-13; 28-31
GOD said to Moses and Aaron while still in Egypt, "This month is to be the first month of the year for you. Address the whole community of Israel; tell them that on the tenth of this month each man is to take a lamb for his family, one lamb to a house. If the family is too small for a lamb, then share it with a close neighbor, depending on the number of persons involved. Be mindful of how much each person will eat. Your lamb must be a healthy male, one year old; you can select it

from either the sheep or the goats. Keep it penned until the fourteenth day of this month and then slaughter it—the entire community of Israel will do this—at dusk.

Then take some of the blood and smear it on the two doorposts and the lintel of the houses in which you will eat it. You are to eat the meat, roasted in the fire, that night, along with bread, made without yeast, and bitter herbs. Don't eat any of it raw or boiled in water; make sure it's roasted—the whole animal, head, legs, and innards. Don't leave any of it until morning; if there are leftovers, burn them in the fire.

And here is how you are to eat it: Be fully dressed with your sandals on and your stick in your hand. Eat in a hurry; it's the Passover to GOD.

I will go through the land of Egypt on this night and strike down every firstborn in the land of Egypt, whether human or animal, and bring judgment on all the gods of Egypt. I am GOD. The blood will serve as a sign on the houses where you live. When I see the blood I will pass over you—no disaster will touch you when I strike the land of Egypt.

The Israelites then went and did what GOD had commanded Moses and Aaron. They did it all.

At midnight GOD struck every firstborn in the land of Egypt, from the firstborn of Pharaoh, who sits on his throne, right down to the firstborn of the prisoner locked up in jail. Also the firstborn of the animals.

Pharaoh and all his servants and everyone else in Egypt

got up during the night and there was loud wailing throughout Egypt. There wasn't a house in which someone wasn't dead.

Pharaoh called in Moses and Aaron that very night and said, "Get out of here - you and your Israelites! Go worship GOD on your own terms. And yes, take your sheep and cattle as you've insisted, but go. And bless me."

ALL:
Blessed is He who keeps His promise to Israel. For the Lord premeditated the end of the bondage, fulfilling what He said to Abraham in the Covenant.

NEXT PERSON IN ROTATION: *Genesis 15:13-14*
"God said to Abram, "Know this: your descendants will live as outsiders in a land not theirs; they'll be enslaved and beaten down for 400 years. Then I'll punish their slave masters; your offspring will march out of there loaded with plunder. But not you; you'll have a long and full life and die a good and peaceful death. Not until the fourth generation will your descendants return here."

ALL:
The Lord brought us out of Egypt.

NEXT PERSON:
"The Israelites had lived in Egypt 430 years. At the end of the 430 years, to the very day, GOD's entire army left Egypt. GOD kept watch all night, watching over the Israelites as he brought them out of Egypt. Because GOD kept watch, all Israel for all generations will honor

GOD by keeping watch this night for generations to come." *(Exodus 12:40-42)*

Exodus 13:17-22: God Leads Israel by a Pillar of Cloud by Day & Fire by Night
It so happened that after Pharaoh released the people, God didn't lead them by the road through the land of the Philistines, which was the shortest route, for God thought, "If the people encounter war, they'll change their minds and go back to Egypt." So God led the people on the wilderness road, looping around to the Red Sea. The Israelites left Egypt in military formation.

Moses took the bones of Joseph with him, for Joseph had made the Israelites solemnly swear to do it, saying, "God will surely hold you accountable, so make sure you bring my bones from here with you." They moved on from Succoth and then camped at Etham at the edge of the wilderness. God went ahead of them in a Pillar of Cloud during the day to guide them on the way, and at night in a Pillar of Fire to give them light; thus they could travel both day and night. The Pillar of Cloud by day and the Pillar of Fire by night never left the people.

Exodus 14: God Parts the Red Sea
God spoke to Moses: "Tell the Israelites to turn around and make camp at Pi Hahiroth, between Migdol and the sea. Camp on the shore of the sea opposite Baal Zephon. "Pharaoh will think, 'The Israelites are lost; they're confused. The wilderness has closed in on them.' Then I'll make Pharaoh's heart stubborn again and he'll chase after them. And I'll use Pharaoh and his army to put my Glory on display. Then the Egyptians will realize that I am God." And that's what happened.

When the king of Egypt was told that the people were gone, he and his servants changed their minds. They said, "What have we done, letting Israel, our slave labor, go free?" So he had his chariots harnessed up and got his army together. He took six hundred of his best chariots, with the rest of the Egyptian chariots and their drivers coming along.

God made Pharaoh king of Egypt stubborn, determined to chase the Israelites as they walked out on him without even looking back. The Egyptians gave chase and caught up with them where they had made camp by the sea—all Pharaoh's horse-drawn chariots and their riders, all his foot soldiers there at Pi Hahiroth opposite Baal Zephon.

As Pharaoh approached, the Israelites looked up and saw them— Egyptians! Coming at them! They were terrified and cried out to the Lord. They told Moses, "Weren't the cemeteries large enough in Egypt so that you had to take us out here in the wilderness to die? What have you done to us, taking us out of Egypt? Back in Egypt didn't we tell you this would happen? Didn't we tell you,

'Leave us alone here in Egypt - we're better off as slaves in Egypt than as corpses in the wilderness.'"

Moses spoke to the people: "Don't be afraid. Stand firm and watch God do his work of salvation for you today. Take a good look at the Egyptians today for you're never going to see them again. God will fight the battle for you. You need only to be still!"

...The angel of God that had been leading the camp of Israel now shifted and got behind them. And the Pillar of Cloud that had been in front also shifted to the rear. The Cloud was now between the camp of Egypt and the camp of Israel. The Cloud enshrouded one camp in darkness and flooded the other with light. The two camps didn't come near each other all night. Then Moses stretched out his hand over the sea and God, with a terrific east wind all night long, made the sea go back. He made the sea dry ground. The seawaters split.

The Israelites walked through the sea on dry ground with the waters a wall to the right and to the left. The Egyptians came after them in full pursuit, every horse and chariot and driver of Pharaoh racing into the middle of the sea. It was now the morning watch. God looked down from the Pillar of Fire and Cloud on the Egyptian army and threw them into a panic. He clogged the wheels of their chariots; they were stuck in the mud. The Egyptians said, "Run from Israel! God is fighting on their side and against Egypt!"

God said to Moses, "Stretch out your hand over the sea and the waters will come back over the Egyptians, over their chariots, over their horsemen." Moses stretched his hand out over the sea: As the day broke and the Egyptians were running, the sea returned to its place as before. God dumped the Egyptians in the middle of the sea. The waters returned, drowning the chariots and riders of Pharaoh's army that had chased after Israel into the sea. Not one of them survived.

But the Israelites walked right through the middle of the

sea on dry ground, the waters forming a wall to the right and to the left. God delivered Israel that day from the oppression of the Egyptians. And Israel looked at the Egyptian dead, washed up on the shore of the sea, and realized the tremendous power that God brought against the Egyptians. The people were in reverent awe before God and trusted in God and his servant Moses.

After witnessing this great miracle, Moses and the people sang a song of praise to God for their deliverance, and Miriam led the women in a joyous dance...

And so began Israel's journey from slavery to freedom, from sadness to joy, from being strangers in Egypt to becoming a great nation. The crossing of the sea represented the birth of a new nation, redeemed by the blood of lambs.

Moses told the people, "Remember the day which you came out from Egypt, out of the house of slavery, for by a strong hand the Lord brought you out of that place. You shall tell your son on that day, 'It is because of what the Lord did for me when I came out of Egypt.' You shall therefore keep this statue at its appointed time from year to year. Now let us all say:

ALL:
Amen

PRAISE GOD: "DAYENU"

In light of all that God has done for us, we surely should express our heartfelt gratitude and give thanks for our salvation. It is customary to sing some verses of the ancient Hebrew song Dayenu (DI – AYE – NUE) which means "it would have been enough for us"):

Many Jewish families sing this in Hebrew. We will read it in English, you can also download it and sing along. It's a catchy tune!

NEXT PERSON IN ROTATION BEGINS:
Had He brought us out from Egypt and not executed judgment against them, DAYEINU!
Had He executed judgment against them and not done justice to their idols, DAYEINU!
Had He done justice to their idols and not slain their first-born DAYEINU!
Had He slain their first-born and not given us their property DAYEINU!
Had He given us their property, and not divided the sea for us DAYEINU!
It would have been enough for us "if through Jesus, we received eternal salvation and not received His Holy Spirit. DAYEINU!
Had He given us His Holy Spirit and not bestowed us with the fruit of the Spirit. It would have been enough for us. DAYEINU!
Had He bestowed us with the fruit of the Spirit and not given us His peace. It would have been enough for us. DAYEINU!

[In the Jewish Seder Guide there are 26 verses to this song. I say DAYEINU at eight!]
ALL:
Dayeinu! Amen!

The Host holds up or refers to the shank bone on the Seder Plate, then reads:
The Passover Sacrifice, the lamb, which our fathers used to eat at the time when the temple still stood – what was the reason for it?

NEXT PERSON IN ROTATION:
Because the Lord, passed over the houses of our Fathers in Egypt. As it is said, It is the sacrifice of the Lord's Passover, for He passed over the homes of the Children of Israel, when he struck the Egyptians; He passed over our homes and did not come in to destroy us.

The children of Israel were told how to protect themselves from the last plague – the plague of death. Each family was to take a lamb, kill it and drain the blood into a basin; and then take hyssop and dip it in the blood and apply the blood to their doorposts – along the top and sides.

During this part of the Seder you can have the children or your group place red streamers around the doorposts as a visual to remember year after year.

As believers we know Jesus shed His blood as a final sacrifice for us. John the Baptist said, "Behold the Lamb of God who takes away the sins of the world!" (John 1:29)

Jewish Believers say the Passover Feast was an enactment or a rehearsal each year so the Jewish people would know and recognize the Messiah when He came. Passover pointed to Jesus.

In Exodus 12, we read what was to happen in Jerusalem on Passover. On the 10th of Nisan, the Passover Lamb was led through the Sheep Gate for its journey to the temple. The lamb was then taken to the temple where it was kept four days under close observation. (Ex 12:3&6) According to Jewish tradition there were several tests performed on the lambs to ensure it's purity.

On the 14th day, after it was declared pure, it was placed on the altar to remain there until 3p.m. for the sacrifice. Not one bone was to be broken.

The similarities between the Passover Lamb and Jesus, the Lamb of God, are hard to miss! Jesus entered Jerusalem on Palm Sunday, the 10th of Nisan (4 days before Passover). He was closely watched and questioned by the religious leaders during those four days. The priests tried to trap him that week while He taught in the temple, but they couldn't do it. They arrested him in the night and early Friday morning, Pilate declared Him INNOCENT – PURE.

Jesus had done NOTHING deserving of death.

On Good Friday, because it was almost sundown – and Jewish Sabbath begins at sundown - they broke the legs of the other criminals on the cross but not Jesus's legs, because at 3p.m. – the same time of the Passover sacrifice - He gave up the ghost and died.

This is the story Jewish Believers and Christians tell at Passover. Jesus is the Passover Lamb, who takes away the sins of the world.

"The blood will serve as a sign on the houses where you live. When I see the blood I will pass over you - no disaster will touch you when I strike the land of Egypt." *(Exodus 12:13)*

But why did the children of Israel need to be protected against the angel of death who was sent out to execute judgment on the Egyptians? This is the only plague that required Israel to do something. The answer is found throughout the Bible, "Indeed, there is no one on earth who is righteous, no one who does what is right and never sins." *(Ecclesiastes 7:20)*. "The one who sins is the one who will die." *(Ezekiel 18:20)*.

Everyone who fails to live up to the moral law of God is guilty and has to pay with his or her life. In the Old Testament Law, the blood of an unblemished lamb became the symbol of an innocent life covering the guilty life from the eyes of a Holy and just God. "When I see the blood I will pass over you."

The prophet Isaiah wrote about the Messiah when he said, "We all, like sheep, have gone astray, each of us has turned to our own way;   and the Lord has laid ON HIM the iniquity of us all. He was oppressed and afflicted, yet he did not open his mouth;   he was led like a lamb to the slaughter   and as a sheep before its shearers is silent,   so he did not open his mouth." *(Isaiah 53:5-7)*

John, the Baptist, seeing Jesus said, "Behold, the Lamb of God who takes away the sins of the world." *(John*

1:29)

I Corinthians 5:7 says, "For Christ, our Passover lamb, has been sacrificed." God transferred our sin to the sinless Christ Jesus. By believing and trusting in Him, we are forgiven and saved! In Him Passover is fulfilled and salvation has come to The World.

The Host lifts his cup of wine and says...

HOST:
Therefore, it is our duty to thank, praise, glorify, extol, bless, exalt and adore Him Who did all of these miracles for our fathers and for us. He has brought us from slavery to freedom, from sorrow to joy, from mourning to festive days, from darkness to a great light, and from subjection to redemption.

Let us then recite before Him a new song.

Host sets down his cup of wine without drinking it.

ALL STAND and recite Psalm 114, continue rotating individual readings.

ALL:
HALLELUJAH, praise the Lord!

READING:
After Israel left Egypt, The house of Jacob left those barbarians behind;

ALL:
All Judea was made his sanctuary: Israel his dominion.

114

READING:
The sea looked and fled: The Jordan river was turned back.

ALL:
The mountains skipped like rams: And the hills like the lambs of the flock.

READING:
What ailed you, O sea, that you turned and ran away: And you, O Jordan, that you were turned back?

ALL:
You mountains, that you skipped like rams: And you hills like lambs of the flock?

READING:
At the presence of the Lord the earth was moved: At the presence of the God of Jacob:

ALL:
He turned the rock into pools of water: And the stony hill into fountains of waters. HALLELUJAH, Praise the Lord!

All are seated.

THE BLESSING OF THE CEREMONIAL FOOD

The Host takes the cup in his hand and says:
Blessed are You, O Lord our God, King of the Universe, Who has redeemed us and our fathers from Egypt, and has permitted us to live until this night, to partake of

the unleavened bread and the bitter herbs.

HOSTESS:
Blessed are you, O God, for you have, in mercy
supplied all our needs. You have given us Jesus,
forgiveness for sin, life abundant and life everlasting.
Hallelujah!

ALL:
Blessed are You, O Lord our God, King of the universe,
Who creates the fruit of the vine.

One of the key customs at Passover is to relate
personally to the story as though you, yourself came up
out of Egypt. As Christians, we can relate – we were
slaves to our sins and in Jesus we are set FREE! As we
drink the second cup, we thank God for delivering us
with His mighty hand!

All drink the second cup of wine, The Cup of
Deliverance.

With the final plague – the death of the firstborn, Israel
was free! With Jesus's death on the cross, we are free.
For Discussion (Optional): How has Jesus set you free?
What's your story? Have you or your family
experienced miracles? Those who want to share, may
do so here.
Now, the leader lifts up the stack of Matzah,.

HOST: Blessed are You, O Lord our God, King of the
Universe, Who brings forth bread from the earth.

Now, the Host takes the bottom matzah and passes it to

all at the table. Each person should break off <u>FIVE</u> olive size pieces.

Once everyone has gotten their 5 pieces of bread, hold one piece up and ALL say:
Blessed are You, O Lord our God, King of the Universe, Who has sanctified us by Your commandments and has commanded us to eat the unleavened bread.

The unleavened bread, the bread of affliction represents Jesus. It is made of only flour and water – no yeast – a symbol of sin. After the dough is flattened, before baking, it is pierced and striped with a pointed tool to keep it from bubbling during the cooking process.

Jesus was sinless – pure. His hands and feet were pierced with nails on the cross. His side pierced with the spear.

"But he was pierced for our transgressions, he was crushed for our sins;   the punishment that brought us peace was on him,   and by his wounds we are healed." *(Isaiah 53:5)*

All eat the bread.

We eat bitter herbs to recall that the Egyptians embittered the lives of our fathers, as it is written: "And the Egyptians hated the children of Israel, and afflicted them and mocked them: And they made their life bitter with hard works in clay, and brick, and with all manner of service wherewith they were overcharged in the works of the earth." *(Exodus 1:13-14)* When we eat the

117

bitter herbs, we remember the sorrow, persecution, and suffering of our life in bondage. As the bitter herbs bring tears to our eyes, so we remember the affliction of our people.

As Christians, eating the bitter herbs reminds us of our lives before we knew Jesus as Savior. The bitter herbs represent the bitter cup our Lord tasted on our behalf. The horseradish brings tears to our eyes as we taste it and remember.

ALL:
Blessed are You, O Lord our God, King of the Universe, Who has sanctified us by Your commandments and has commanded us concerning the eating of bitter herbs.

Dip one piece of matzah in the horseradish. All eat the bread and horseradish together.

The Haroset represents the mortar the Israelites were forced to make under Pharaoh's taskmasters. The sweetness reminds us of the hope they had in freedom. For us, it reminds us that even in the toughest circumstances they are sweetened by our hope in God.

Dip the third piece of matzah in the haroset. All eat the bread and haroset.

READING:
In the days of the Second Temple, an argument broke out among the sages. The sage Hillel thought the matzah and bitter herbs should be eaten together; however, other sages thought they should be eaten separately.

Therefore, the tradition began to do it both ways – we first eat the bitter herbs separately, then together with the Hillel Sandwich.

Now, place horseradish and haroset between two pieces of unleavened bread (The Hillel Sandwich).

All eat the Hillel sandwich.
This concludes the Ceremonial Meal.
THE PASSOVER SUPPER is now served. Set aside your Seder Guides and enjoy the meal. Host blesses the meal and the time together. Your key goal here is to spend time together focused on the true meaning of Easter – Jesus came and became our Passover Lamb.

HOST BLESSES THE MEAL:
Blessed are You, O Lord our God, King of the Universe, Who has sanctified us with His commandments, and commanded us to eat the Passover Meal.

THE CUP OF REDEMPTION, The Third Cup is Poured: "I will redeem you"

By this time in the meal, the lost Afikomen should have been found and a reward given by the Host.

The host unwraps the Afikomen and breaks it into small pieces and distributes it to all present.

NEXT PERSON IN THE ROTATION:
It is customary to end the Passover meal by eating this final piece of unleavened bread that was 'lost' – the Afikoman. The word "Afikoman" is Greek and means

"the coming one."

This is the broken piece of matzah that was hidden away earlier this evening. When this middle piece was broken at the start of our Seder, it symbolized the breaking of the body of the Son of God. This half was separated and wrapped in linen, foreshadowing the wrapping of Christ's body after the crucifixion. When the broken and wrapped bread was hidden, this symbolized Jesus's burial. When the Afikomen is found and redeemed, this represents His resurrection.

For it is written, "During the meal, Jesus took and blessed the bread, broke it, and gave it to His disciples: Take, eat. This is my body." *(Matthew 26:26)*

The Bible also says, "Let me go over with you again exactly what goes on in the Lord's Supper and why it is so centrally important. I received my instructions from the Master himself and passed them on to you. The Master, Jesus, on the night of his betrayal, took bread. Having given thanks, he broke it and said, this is my body, broken for you. Do this to remember me." *(I Corinthians 11:23-24)*

All hold the bread in their hands while the host says:

HOST:
This broken bread represents Jesus, the Messiah's body that was broken for you on the cross.

Blessed are you, LORD our God, King of the universe, Who brings forth bread from the earth.

HOSTESS:
Jesus also said, "I am the bread of life." *(John 6:48)* and "I am the living bread that came down from heaven. Whoever eats this bread will live forever. This bread is my flesh, which I will give for the life of the world." *(John 6:51)*

We pause in silence and consider the bread in our hands and what it represents. Leaven is a symbol of sin, and Jesus was sinless. See the stripes and pierced holes in the matzah. Jesus was striped by a Roman's whip and pierced by nails on the cross and a soldier's spear.

HOST:
The Afikoman memorializes Jesus's sacrifice of atonement for our sins so that we might have peace with God. When we eat the broken matzah, we remember that He allowed his body to be broken as our sacrifice for sin, and we thank God that He allowed His body to be the Lamb of God who came to bear the sins of the world – once and for all.

We will add the additional blessing, thanking the LORD God of Israel for providing us with the true Bread from Heaven, His beloved Son:
Blessed are You, LORD our God, King of the universe, who brings forth the True Bread from Heaven. Let us bless the Lord.

If you have believers at your table, you may conduct The Lord's Supper here. If there are non-believers, you can just continue and not call it The Lord's Super.

All eat the bread

The Third cup of wine is poured now.

HOST:
Then he took the Third Cup of Wine – the Cup of Redemption.

I will Redeem you with an outstretched arm. (Exodus 6:6)

Surely, the arm of the Lord is not too short to save. (Isaiah 59:1)

It is our own righteousness that that falls short. Therefore, His own arm brought him salvation, and his own righteousness sustained him. (Isaiah 59:16)

Matthew 26:27-29: Then he took a cup, and when he had given thanks, he gave it to them, saying, "Drink from it, all of you. This is my blood of the covenant, which is poured out for many for the forgiveness of sins. I tell you, I will not drink from this fruit of the vine from now on until that day when I drink it new with you in my Father's kingdom."

Just as the blood of the lamb brought salvation in Egypt, so Jesus's atoning death brings salvation to all who believe.

Blessed are you, O Lord our God, ruler of the universe, who creates the fruit of the vine. Let us gratefully drink.

All drink the third cup of Redemption.
For Discussion (Optional): Consider The Lord's Supper,

what are your thoughts as you eat the bread and drink the wine/juice?

The Fourth Cup: The Cup of Restoration: I will take you as MY people and I will be your God.

The fourth cup is filled.

Psalm 118
Give thanks to the Lord, for he is good; His love endures forever.

Let Israel say: "His love endures forever." Let the house of Aaron say: "His love endures forever." Let those who fear the Lord say: "His love endures forever."

When hard pressed, I cried to the Lord;   he brought me into a spacious place. The Lord is with me; I will not be afraid. What can mere mortals do to me? The Lord is with me; he is my helper. I look in triumph on my enemies.

It is better to take refuge in the Lord than to trust in humans. It is better to take refuge in the Lord   than to trust in princes. All the nations surrounded me,   but in the name of the Lord I cut them down. They surrounded me on every side, but in the name of the Lord I cut them down.

They swarmed around me like bees, but they were consumed as quickly as burning thorns; in the name of the Lord I cut them down. I was pushed back and about to fall, but the Lord helped me. The Lord is my strength and my defense; he has become my salvation.

Shouts of joy and victory resound in the tents of the righteous: "The Lord's right hand has done mighty things! The Lord's right hand is lifted high; the Lord's right hand has done mighty things!" I will not die but live, and will proclaim what the Lord has done. The Lord has chastened me severely, but he has not given me over to death. Open for me the gates of the righteous; I will enter and give thanks to the Lord. This is the gate of the Lord through which the righteous may enter. I will give you thanks, for you answered me; you have become my salvation.

The stone the builders rejected has become the cornerstone; the Lord has done this, and it is marvelous in our eyes. The Lord has done it this very day; let us rejoice today and be glad.

Lord, save us! Lord, grant us success!

Blessed is he who comes in the name of the Lord. From the house of the Lord we bless you. The Lord is God, and he has made his light shine on us. With boughs in hand, join in the festal procession up to the horns of the altar.

You are my God, and I will praise you; you are my God, and I will exalt you.
Give thanks to the Lord, for he is good; his love endures forever!

Let everything that has breath Praise the Lord! *(Psalm 150:6)*

THE CUP OF ELIJAH
Have the children open the front door.

HOSTESS:
Tradition holds that we save an extra place for Elijah.
The door is open for Elijah to arrive and announce that
the Messiah has come. Jesus spoke of John the Baptist
as
His forerunner saying:
(Mark 9:11-13; Matthew 11:13-15) And they asked
him (Jesus), "Why do the teachers of the law say that
Elijah must come first? " Jesus replied, "To be sure,
Elijah does come first, and restores all things. Why then
is it written that the Son of Man must suffer much and
be rejected? But I tell you, Elijah has come, and they
have done to him everything they wished, just as it is
written about him." For all the Prophets and the Law
prophesied until John. And if you are willing to accept
it, he is the Elijah who was to come. He who has ears,
let him hear.
"Elijah has come" This was true in the person of John
the Baptist.
So please close the door and be seated. Elijah and the
Messiah have already come and we now await His
triumphant return as King of Kings and Lord of Lords!

During the Last Supper, Jesus did not drink the fourth
cup (the cup of Restoration), but promised to do so
with His disciples in the Kingdom to come. This cup
looks forward to the day when Jesus comes back for
His bride, the church for the Wedding Supper of the
Lamb.

Revelation 19:6-9, excerpts: "Then I heard what sounded like a great multitude... shouting: "Halleluah! For our Lord God Almight reigns. Let us rejoice and be glad... For the wedding of the lamb has come, and his bride has made herself ready"... Then the angel said to me, "Write this: Blessed are those who are invited to the wedding supper of the Lamb!""

The Passover is central to the overarching story of God's Redemptive Plan for the world. It begins with Passover where He saved His people Israel, it moves to the Lord's Supper where Christ redeems sinners. Currently, we are between Feasts – the Lord's Supper and the Wedding Supper of the Lamb.

Revelations 21:1-4, excerpts: Then I saw a new Heaven and a new earth, for the first heaven and the first earth had passed away... I saw the Holy City, the New Jerusalem, coming down out of heaven from God... And I heard a loud voice from the throne saying, "Look! God's dwelling place is now among the people, and He will dwell with them. They will be His people, and God Himself will be with them and be their God."

The 4th Cup, The Cup of Restoration - "I will take you as my people and I will be your God."

This cup looks forward to the day when Jesus comes back to take us to be with Him and to restore His Kingdom.

All raise their cups and say,

We Praise You, O Lord our God, King of the Universe, Who has created the fruit of the vine.

All drink the fourth cup.

HOST: Our Passover Seder is now complete. Lord, grant us peace that we may do your will.

The Host says a final blessing:
The Lord bless you and keep you, The Lord make his face shine upon you and be gracious to you, The Lord turn his face toward you and give you peace!
Amen!

This concludes the Passover Seder.

Seder Guide: Abridged

INSTRUCTIONS on How To Use This Seder Guide:
This ABRIDGED Seder Guide should be used as a tool to help inspire as well as enhance your Seder experience. By focusing and learning about Passover we see how Jesus fulfills this ancient celebrated feast.

As you gather your group together to participate in this Passover Feast be sure everyone has a copy of this abridged guide (starting on the next page). You will read through this document rotating from person to person. Instructions are written throughout feel free to read aloud or not as you go along.

Designate a host and hostess for your group, as each have specific tasks and help lead and guide the Seder. Keep in mind, Passover is, by tradition, an inclusive holiday and all are invited to participate – you don't have to know what to do or what comes next because the guide will simply walk you through it!

Lighting of the Candles – the Hostess lights the candles to begin the Seder. While lighting the candles she says a prayer:

HOSTESS:
Blessed are You, O Lord our God, King of the universe,
Who has sanctified us by Your commandments
And commanded us to kindle the festival lights.

Blessed are You, O Lord our God, King of the universe,
Who sanctified us with His commandments,
And commanded us to be a light to the nations
And Who gave to us Jesus our Messiah the Light of the world.
May our home be consecrated, O God,
By the Light of Your countenance,
Shining upon us in blessing and bringing us peace.

ALL: AMEN

If you prefer to say your own prayer here, that's OK. The primary purpose here is to initiate the lighting of the candles, recognizing Jesus as the Light of the world, kicking off your Passover Seder and blessing your time together.

The Washing of Hands – Place wet naps near each place setting for the "washing" of hands. You may recall in the Last Supper when Jesus washed the feet of the disciples, it was probably at this point that He did that. Read this verse while "washing" hands.

ALL "WASH" HANDS

PERSON TO THE LEFT OF THE HOSTESS READS,
THEN ROTATE EVERY PARAGRAPH:
"After that, he poured water into a basin and began to
wash his disciples' feet, drying them with the towel that
was wrapped around him... When he had finished
washing their feet, he put on his clothes and returned
to his place. "Do you understand what I have done for
you?" he asked them. "You call me 'Teacher' and
'Lord,' and rightly so, for that is what I am. Now that I,
your Lord and Teacher, have washed your feet, you
also should wash one another's feet. I have set you an
example that you should do as I have done for you."
(John 13:5, 12-15)

NEXT PERSON READS:
Review the Special Order of the Seder – During the
Seder we drink 4 cups of wine or grape juice. These
cups have meaning to the Jewish people. The Seder is
divided into 4 parts according to the 4 cups of
wine/juice. The 4 Cups represent the following:
Cup of Sanctification: "I will bring you out." Readings
are focused on God separating Israel as His chosen
people. What a great parallel for us as Christians, we
are called out – to be separate from the world around
us.

Cup of Deliverance: "I will free you." During this time
in the ceremony the focus is on the plagues and telling
the story of Israel's deliverance. We all have a story
too. Here, we remember and share the things He has
done for us – He delivered us from the slavery of sin.
After the second cup and readings, we will break for
the Passover meal.

Cup of Redemption: "I will redeem you to myself." The third cup reminds the children of Israel that they are His chosen, redeemed people by the blood of Lambs. This Cup of Redemption, taken after the meal, is where Jesus instituted the Lord's Supper. He changed the Passover Seder to something new. Here He instituted a new covenant. It was at this point in the Seder we are to remember His blood shed and His body broken for us when we eat the Bread and drink the Wine. He Redeemed us. In the Old Testament Passover He saved His People, Israel. In the Lord's Supper Jesus redeems the World once and for all.

Cup of Restoration: "I will take you as my people and I will be your God." This cup looks forward to the great feast we will one day share in Heaven with Jesus. He didn't drink from this 4th cup that night. He's waiting to do that with us at the Marriage Supper of the Lamb.

The four cups represent the promises God made to the children of Israel while they were still in Egypt.

Exodus 6:5-7: "Moreover, I have heard the groaning of the Israelites, whom the Egyptians are enslaving, and I have remembered my covenant. Therefore, say to the Israelites: 'I am the Lord, and I will bring you out from under the yoke of the Egyptians. I will free you from being slaves to them, and I will redeem you with an outstretched arm and with mighty acts of judgment. I will take you as my own people, and I will be your God. Then you will know that I am the Lord your God, who brought you out from under the yoke of the Egyptians."

As Christians we are called out to be separate from the world around us. Jesus delivered us from the slavery of sin when He redeemed us by dying on the cross. We now look forward to His return as King of Kings and Lord of Lords. He will take us as His own and we shall dwell with Him forever.

The Cup of Sanctification – Pour the first glass of wine. I will bring you out.

ALL:
Blessed are You, O Lord our God, King of the Universe, Who creates the fruit of the vine.

After this blessing, all drink the first cup.

Bless the Children: If children are present, this is the time parents place their hands on each of their children's heads and bless them. Again, feel free to say your own prayer over your children. If no children are present, skip to "Dip the Vegetable".
The LORD bless you and keep you;
the LORD make his face shine on you and be gracious to you;
the LORD turn his face toward you and give you peace.
Numbers 6:24-26

Dip the Vegetable: The Seder Plate is passed to all so everyone can take a piece of parsley. All dip the parsley in the salt water, bless it and eat.
The parsley (or green vegetable) symbolizes the growth and fertility of the Jewish people in Egypt. It also recalls their great suffering. We eat parsley dipped in salt

water to remember the tears shed during the time of oppression and slavery in Egypt. For Christians, it represents new life, growing in His word and discipleship in Jesus.

All take the parsley, dip it in the salt-water, and say:

ALL:
Blessed are You, O Lord our God, King of the Universe, Who creates the fruit of the soil.

All eat the parsley.

The Matzah: The Host lifts the 3 Matzah, then takes the Middle Matzah and breaks it in two. He places the larger piece back with the others (still in the middle) and wraps the smaller piece in a cloth that is hidden for the children to find. If there are no children, just set this off to the side for later use.

The Middle Matzah that is removed is called the Afikomen. We will discuss this more following the meal.

HOST: "This is the bread of our affliction our fathers ate in the land of Egypt. Let all who are hungry come and eat. Let all who are in want come and celebrate the Passover with us. May it be God's will to redeem us from all evil and from all slavery."

As Believers in Christ, we too celebrate this Seder. Jesus celebrated Passover all the years of His life including the night before he died. As we go through this Seder, consider your salvation and how the Lord, our God rescued us from the slavery of sin into eternal life and freedom in Jesus Christ.

The 4 Questions: The youngest child/person at the table asks the questions below.

"Why is this night different from all other nights?

On all other nights we eat either leavened or unleavened bread, but on this night why only unleavened bread?

On all other nights we eat vegetables and herbs of all kinds; why on this night do we eat only bitter herbs?

On all other nights we never think of dipping herbs in water or in anything else; why on this night do we dip the parsley in salt water and the bitter herbs in charoset?

On all other nights we eat either sitting upright or reclining; why on this night do we recline as we partake of the four cups of wine?

Answering the Questions (All rotate answering the Questions): "I'm glad you've asked these questions.

Exodus 12:26-27: And when your children ask you, 'What does this ceremony mean to you?' then tell them, 'It is the Passover sacrifice to the Lord, who passed over the houses of the Israelites in Egypt and spared our homes when he struck down the Egyptians.'" Then the people bowed down and worshiped.

Why do we eat only matzah? When Pharaoh released our forefathers from Egypt they were forced to leave in great haste. They had little time to bake their bread and could not wait for it to rise. The sun beat down on the dough as they carried it along, and baked it into unleavened bread called Matzah. For Christians when we share in the bread of Passover and The Lord's Supper, we share in Christ who was broken on our behalf. He is the true Bread, the Bread of Life.

Why do we eat bitter herbs? So that we are reminded that our forefathers were slaves in Egypt and their lives were made very bitter. We remember the bitterness of sin and our lives before Jesus. We were slaves to our sin, but Jesus set us free.

Why do we dip the herbs tonight? The parsley reminds us of the hyssop used to place the blood of the lamb upon the doorposts and lintels. The salt water reminds us of the Red Sea and of the tears shed while they were in bondage. The sweet charoset reminds us that our forefathers were able to withstand bitter slavery because it was sweetened by the hope of freedom. For us, it reminds us that even in the toughest circumstances they are sweetened knowing we can trust and hope in the Lord our God.

Why do we recline at the table? It is because reclining was a sign of a free man long ago, and since our forefathers were freed on this night, we recline at the table. Jesus said, "Come to me, all you who are weary and burdened, and I will give you rest." Matthew 11:28

The Telling: (All get your Bibles and rotate reading the story of the Exodus alternating sections or paragraphs in the Bible. Exodus Chapter 12 is the primary chapter read. We suggest you use a newer translation like NIV, ESV or NLT.)

For Discussion (Optional): How has God called you to be separate from the world around you?

The Second Cup, the Cup of Deliverance is poured after Exodus 12 is read: "I will rescue you." God rescued Israel with wondrous signs!

The Plagues: Here, the plagues are recited. All dip their finger in the second cup of wine or juice and recite each of the plagues while dotting the edge of each plate.

ALL: Blood, Frogs, Gnats, Flies, Sickness, Boils, Hail, Locusts, Darkness, Death of the Firstborn. (Your plate should have dots of wine/juice along the edge).

We do this because our joy is diminished because of the suffering of the Egyptians. We should never take joy in the sufferings of others; therefore our second cup isn't completely full.

Pesach (Pay-sok) Passover/the Lamb): The host holds the shank bone and recites:

HOST: The Passover Sacrifice, the lamb, which our fathers ate, was as an offering unto God that spared them from the angel of death.

Ex 12:27: "Then tell them, 'It is the Passover sacrifice to the Lord, who passed over the houses of the Israelites in Egypt and spared our homes when he struck down the Egyptians.'" Then the people bowed down and worshiped."

During this part of the Seder you can have the children or your group place red streamers around the doorposts as a visual to remember year after year.

As believers we know Jesus shed His blood as a final sacrifice for us. John the Baptist said, "Behold the Lamb of God who takes away the sins of the world!" (John 1:29)

Jewish Believers say the Passover Feast was an enactment or a rehearsal each year so the Jewish people would know and recognize the Messiah when He came. Passover pointed to Jesus.

In Exodus 12, we read what was to happen in Jerusalem on Passover. On the 10th of Nisan, the Passover Lamb was led through the Sheep Gate for its journey to the temple. The lamb was then taken to the temple where it was kept four days under close observation. (Ex 12:3&6) According to Jewish tradition there were several tests performed on the lambs to ensure it's purity. On the 14th day, after it was declared pure, it was placed on the altar to remain there until 3p.m. for the sacrifice. Not one bone was to be broken.

The similarities between the Passover Lamb and Jesus, the Lamb of God, are hard to miss! Jesus entered Jerusalem on Palm Sunday, the 10th of Nisan (4 days before Passover). He was closely watched and questioned by the religious leaders during those four days. The priests tried to trap him that week while He taught in the temple, but they couldn't do it. They arrested him in the night and early Friday morning, Pilate declared Him INNOCENT – PURE. Jesus had done NOTHING deserving of death.

On Good Friday, because it was almost sundown – and Jewish Sabbath begins at sundown - they broke the legs of the other criminals on the cross but not Jesus's legs, because at 3p.m. – the same time of the Passover sacrifice - He gave up the ghost and died.

This is the story Jewish Believers and Christians tell at Passover. Jesus is the Passover Lamb, who takes away the sins of the world.

All raise the SECOND cup: "the Cup of Deliverance," the host/hostess says a prayer of thanksgiving to God for delivering His people from the Egyptians and for saving us. Blessed are you, O God, for you have, in mercy supplied all our needs. You have given us Jesus, forgiveness for sin, life abundant and life everlasting. Hallelujah!

With the final plague – the death of the firstborn, Israel was free! With Jesus's death on the cross, we are free.

We offer praise to God for His Deliverance! In typical Jewish homes, families sing a song called Dayenu (It would have been enough).

For Discussion (Optional): How has Jesus set you free?

What's your story? What miracles have you experienced in your own life? Those who want to share, may do so here.

One of the key customs at Passover is to relate personally to the story as though you, yourself came up out of Egypt. As Christians, we can relate – we were slaves to our sins and in Jesus we are set FREE! As we drink the second cup, we thank God for delivering us with a mighty hand!

All drink the second cup.
Now, the leader lifts up the top Matzah, the bread of affliction, and passes it to all. All should take 4 pieces of olive-sized matzah. The Host says a prayer over the bread and recites:

"Blessed are you , O Lord our God, ruler of the universe, who brings forth bread from the earth"

This is the bread of affliction.

All eat one piece of Matzah together.

The leader lifts up the Bitter Herbs. Life was full of sorrow, persecution and suffering under the Egyptians. Our lives were bitter before we knew the salvation of the Lord.

All place take the second matzah and place the bitter herbs (horseradish) on it and eat.
With the remaining two pieces of matzah, make a "sandwich" by placing the charoset (apple, nut mixture) with the bitter herbs between the two pieces.

Called the Hillel Sandwich.

The Hillel Sandwich reminds us that though our slavery (to sin) was indeed bitter, our redemption (in Jesus) is sweeter still. Let us combine the unleavened bread, the charoset and the bitter herbs and eat them together and remember.

All eat the Hillel sandwich.

This concludes the Ceremonial Meal.

The Passover Supper is now served. Set aside your Seder Guides and enjoy the meal. Host blesses the meal and the time together. Your key goal here is to spend time together focused on the true meaning of Easter – Jesus came and became our Passover Lamb.

The Third Cup is Poured, The Cup of Redemption: "I will redeem you"

By this time in the meal, the lost Afikomen should have been found and a reward given. It must be redeemed, just like WE must be redeemed for a cost.

This Afikomen is then broken and distributed to all.

This is the broken piece of matzah that was hidden away earlier this evening. When this piece was broken at the start of our Seder, it was wrapped in a cloth (a shroud), hidden (buried) and finally for the Seder to end, it must be brought back, found and redeemed.

Matthew 26:26: While they were eating, Jesus took

bread, and when he had given thanks, he broke it and gave it to his disciples, saying, "Take and eat; this is my body."

This is where Jesus instituted the Lord's Supper. After the Passover meal, he took this Afikomen to tell His disciples this was HIS body which is broken for you.

Then he took the Third Cup of Wine, which is served after the meal – the Cup of Redemption - to institute the Lord's Supper.

Matthew 26:27-29: Then he took a cup, and when he had given thanks, he gave it to them, saying, "Drink from it, all of you. This is my blood of the covenant, which is poured out for many for the forgiveness of sins. I tell you, I will not drink from this fruit of the vine from now on until that day when I drink it new with you in my Father's kingdom."

The Cup of Redemption represents God's NEW Covenant, and the blood of Jesus shed for the forgiveness of our sins. Jesus REDEEMED us! It's done!

All eat the afikomen and drink the third cup of Redemption. If you have a table full of Christians, you may observe the Lord's Supper here.

For Discussion (Optional): Consider The Lord's Supper, what are your thoughts as you chew the bread and drink the wine/juice?

The Fourth Cup: The Cup of Restoration: I will take you as MY people and I will be your God.

Read Psalm 118 from your Bibles rotating sections

During the Last Supper, Jesus did not drink the fourth cup (the cup of Restoration), but promised to do so with His disciples in the Kingdom to come. This cup looks forward to the day when Jesus comes back for His bride, the church for the Wedding Supper of the Lamb.

Revelations 19:6-9, excerpts: "Then I heard what sounded like a great multitude... shouting: "Halleluah! For our Lord God Almight reigns. Let us rejoice and be glad... For the wedding of the lamb has come, and his bride has made herself ready"... Then the angel said to me, "Write this: Blessed are those who are invited to the wedding supper of the Lamb!""

The Passover is central to the overarching story of God's Redemptive Plan for the world. It begins with Passover where He saved His people Israel, it moves to the Lord's Supper where Christ redeems sinners. Currently, we are between Feasts – the Lord's Supper and the Wedding Supper of the Lamb.

Revelations 21:1-4, excerpts: Then I saw a new Heaven and a new earth, for the first heaven and the first earth had passed away... I saw the Holy City, the New Jerusalem, coming down out of heaven from God... And I heard a loud voice from the throne saying, "Look! God's dwelling place is now among the people, and He will dwell with them. They will be His people, and God Himself will be with them and be their God."

The 4th Cup, The Cup of Restoration - "I will take you as my people and I will be your God."

This cup looks forward to the day when Jesus comes back to take us to be with Him and to restore His Kingdom.

For Discussion (Optional): Jesus will drink this forth cup with us in Heaven. What do you think it will be like? Using your "holy imagination" consider experiencing The Marriage Supper of the Lamb, seeing and being with Jesus in the kingdom to come.

The End of the Seder
The Host says a final blessing:
The Lord bless you and keep you, The Lord make his face shine upon you and be gracious to you, The Lord turn his face toward you and give you peace!
Amen!

This concludes the Passover Seder.

Seder Guide: Children's

This Seder is designed for children under twelve. Since the Passover Seder is a multi-sensory experience, feel free to experiment with the foods, the Seder order and the way you tell the story. We have included supplementary suggestions for making this meaningful and enjoyable for kids (and therefore their parents!) If you have readers, they can participate in reading the Exodus story and the questions and answers. It's helpful to read the story out of a children's Bible or storybook, since it is usually more concise, or to print off scripture passages in a contemporary translation.

Seder

+ <u>Lighting of the Candles</u>: The hostess/mother lights two white tapered candles; she prays for the Spirit of God to bless her family and be with them as the observe this Passover Seder.

+ <u>Blessing of the Children</u>: The host/father stands with the children and prays individually over each one, asking God's blessing on them.

The traditional prayer is from Numbers 6:24-26 "The Lord bless you and keep you; the Lord make his face shine on you and be gracious to you, the Lord turn his face toward you and give you peace."

+ <u>Story of the Passover</u>: Read Exodus 12 (if you have readers, divide up the story into segments each can read). Or, read the story and have children re-tell it.

+ The Afikomen: The host/father shows the children the three matzah crackers wrapped in cloth. He explains the matzah, the unleavened bread that the Israelites ate as they left Egypt. He breaks the middle matzah in half; wraps one half in another cloth that someone hides in the next room, the other half returns to the matzah bag.

+ The Four Questions:
Host/Father reads: "And when your children ask you, 'What does this ceremony mean to you?' then tell them, 'It is the Passover sacrifice to the Lord, who passed over the houses of the Israelites in Egypt and spared our homes when he struck down the Egyptians" (Ex. 12:26-27.)

Children ask the following questions:
Reader 1:
Question: Why on all other nights do we eat leavened bread, but on this night only unleavened?

Answer: When Pharoah agreed to let the Israelites leave Egypt, they had to leave in a big hurry! They didn't have time for their bread to "rise" (explain.)

Reader 2:
Question: Why on all other nights do we eat all kinds of vegetables but on this night only bitter ones?

Answer: The bad taste reminds us of how bad it felt to be slaves and how bad it feels to disobey God.

Reader 3:
Question: Why on all other nights do we not dip our foods even once, but on this night we dip twice?

Answer: The parsley dipped in salt water reminds us of the branches used to put the lamb's blood over the door and the tears the Israelites cried as the prayed to God for deliverance. The sweet charoset reminds us of the freedom that God gave His people and the sweetness of hope and happiness.

Reader 4:
Question: Why on all other nights do we eat sitting, but tonight we recline?

Answer: We are safe and do not have to leave our homes in a hurry to escape Pharoah like the Israelites did. God has blessed us, we can relax and be safe in our homes as we eat this meal.

+ Pass the Seder plate: Each person takes a small portion. Explain the meaning of the foods and have everyone taste at the same time.

Matzah – a flat bread, an unleavened cracker, the bread the Israelites ate

Grape Juice – represents blood (the Nile turning to blood) and all the plagues. Have children dip little finger in juice and put a dot on the edge of their plate for each plague: blood, frogs, gnats, flies, sickness, boils, hail, locusts, darkness, death of firstborn.

Bitter Herb – represents the tears of slavery

Parsley – represents new life, hope

Salt Water – represents the Red Sea, which the Israelites would miraculously cross

Charoset – represents the sweetness of hope

Egg – represents new life (the egg isn't in the biblical story, but is traditional in Jewish homes)

Lamb bone – represents the Passover Lamb

Optional Plague Activity: In many Jewish homes the children have activities for each of the 10 plagues. If you are also conducting a Seder for the Adults one night this is a good way to include children before they have to retire for bed.

There are Jewish Stores online where you can find "Bags of Plagues" these are fun for the little's too.

Plague	Activity(ies)
Nile turns to blood	Take bottled water and have children drop red food coloring it
Frogs	In some Jewish stores, they sell chocolate frogs. Pass these out to the children and adults as a sweet treat
Gnats/flies	Have the children grind up pepper on their plates to represent gnats and flies
Sickness	They can draw a picture or walk around the table like they are sick. This usually looks like a zombie-walk
Boils	Use red dot stickers and the kids can stick them on themselves and each other
Hail	Indoor firecrackers are fun for this, but kind of messy. There are also bounce balls they can bounce around.
Locusts	The Jewish Bag of Plagues has a good locust in there that we use. If you have toy bugs, those will do fine as well.
Darkness	Blindfold the children and have them lead one another around the table. You can also turn off the lights for a time.
Death of the Firstborn	Use red streamers and tape the "blood of the lamb" over your door and lintels to demonstrate what Israel did to be saved from the final plague.

+ The Lord's Supper: Explain that the night before Jesus' death, He celebrated the Passover with His disciples, eating the same kind of foods the children just ate. At that Seder, Jesus began the Lord's Supper (Communion), which was taking the matzah and juice of the Seder and giving it additional meaning. The bread represents His body and the juice, His blood, given on the cross for us.

Reader 5/6: Read Luke 22:15-20 (depending on readers' age, it is helpful to print out children's translation for them). Emphasize that we "do this" to remember Jesus' death.

+The Afikomen: Remember the half of the matzah that was hidden? Now children go into the next room to look for it. The winner receives a small prize, a piece of candy or $1. There is frequently some bargaining, the children asking for a little more than the host was planning!

+ Conclusion: The Passover is the story of not only Moses and the Israelites, but also of Jesus. We remember his suffering on the cross and that even though we are sinners; Jesus loves us so much that He gave His life for us. We are thankful!
Sing a praise song that children know, one that they choose. This is how Jesus and disciples concluded their Passover, "When they had sung a hymn, they went out…"

Recipes

Green Salad with Strawberries

Recipe from Passover Recipes – Gourmet Kosher Cooking: gourmetforpassover.com

Ingredients:

4 teaspoons strawberry jam

2 tablespoons balsamic vinegar

6 tablespoons extra-virgin olive oil

1 teaspoon kosher salt

¼ teaspoon black pepper

1 pint strawberries, sliced

2 scallions, sliced

½ cup slivered almonds, toasted

4 to 5 cups chopped romaine or mixed greens of any kind

Place jam in a medium bowl and whisk in vinegar then olive oil. Season the dressing with salt and pepper. Add the strawberries, scallions almonds and greens to bowl and toss to coat evenly in dressing.

Matzah Ball Soup
(Recipe by Joyce Goldstein from Fine Cooking Issue 44)

EASY Matzo Ball Soup: Purchase Matzo Ball Soup Mix in the Kosher Section of your grocery store. You can just add the chicken, carrots, celery, etc.

Or you can make it! The matzo balls can be made ahead and then warmed in the broth before serving. To turn this into a more filling meal, you could add cooked chicken, peas, or carrots.

Ingredients:
4 large eggs
1/4 cup rendered chicken fat or fat reserved from the chicken broth, at room temperature
1 tsp. kosher salt
1/4 tsp. freshly ground white pepper
5 oz. (1-1/4 cups) matzo meal
7 cups Chicken Broth
1/4 cup chopped fresh flat-leaf parsley

In a large bowl, whisk together the eggs and 1/3 cup cold water. Add the rendered or reserved chicken fat and whisk until the fat blends in. Mix in the salt and pepper. Gradually but quickly stir in the matzo meal with a spoon; the mixture will be thick and stiff, like muffin batter. Don't overmix. Chill for at least 1 hour or up to 3 hours.

Line a baking sheet with parchment or waxed paper and fill a bowl with cold water. Dip a large soupspoon in the water, and gently scoop up the chilled matzo mixture and shape it with your hands into 12 medium balls (about 1-3/4 inches in diameter) or 18 smaller ones (about 1-1/4 inches in diameter), being careful not to compact them. Put the matzo balls on the lined baking sheet. Cook immediately or refrigerate for up to 1 hour.

To cook the matzo balls, bring 1 or 2 large pots of salted water to a boil. Drop in the matzo balls, cover the pots, and reduce the heat after the water returns to a boil. Simmer, covered, until the matzo balls have doubled in size and have lightened all the way through (cut one in half to check) 30 to 40 minutes; drain. Cooked matzo balls can be held at room temperature for several hours.

To serve, bring the chicken broth to a boil. Taste for salt and pepper. Add the matzo balls and heat until they're hot in the middle, 8 to 10 minutes. With a slotted spoon, put 2 medium or 3 small matzo balls in a warm soup bowl. Ladle in hot broth and sprinkle generously with the parsley. Serve right away.

Grilled Leg of Lamb

(From Gourmet Magazine June 2007)

Ingredients:
4 large garlic cloves
1 1/2 teaspoons salt
2 tablespoons olive oil
1 teaspoon finely grated fresh lemon zest
1 tablespoon fresh lemon juice
5 teaspoons minced fresh thyme
1 teaspoon black pepper
1/2 teaspoon ground allspice
1 (6 1/2- to 7-lb) bone-in leg of lamb, trimmed of all
but a thin layer of fat

Mince garlic, then mash to a paste with salt. Stir
together garlic paste, oil, lemon zest and juice, thyme,
pepper, and allspice. Put lamb, fat side up, in a large
ceramic or glass dish. Using a paring knife, make 1 1/2-
inch-long slits (about 2 inches deep) 2 inches apart all
over leg. Reserve 1 teaspoon thyme mixture and push
remainder into slits, then rub all over with reserved
teaspoon of mixture. Marinate lamb, covered and
chilled, 12 hours.

Let lamb stand at room temperature 30 minutes before
grilling.
Prepare grill for indirect-heat cooking over medium-hot
charcoal (high heat for gas). If using a gas grill, preheat
all burners on high, covered, 10 minutes, then turn off
all burners except burner closest to you.

Oil grill rack, then grill lamb over area with no coals
(or over turned-off burner or burners), covered, without

turning, until thermometer inserted into thickest part of roast (almost to the bone but not touching it) registers 125°F for medium-rare, 1 1/4 to 1 1/2 hours (temperatures in thinner parts of leg may register up to 160°F). To maintain medium-hot charcoal, add more charcoal (about 2 cups) every 15 minutes.

Let lamb stand on a cutting board, uncovered, 30 minutes.

If you aren't able to grill outdoors, lamb can be roasted on a rack set in a large (17- by 11-inch) roasting pan in a 375°F oven, 1 1/4 to 1 1/2 hours.

Roasted Garlic Asparagus
(By Susie Fishbein, Epicurious, March 2011)

Ingredients
1/2 cup extra-virgin olive oil
8 cloves fresh garlic, minced
1 teaspoon onion powder
2 tablespoons fresh finely chopped parsley
2 pounds thin asparagus, ends trimmed
Fleur de sel or coarse sea salt
Freshly ground black pepper

Preheat oven to 400°F.

Line a large jelly-roll pan with parchment paper. Set aside.

In a small pot, heat the oil, garlic, onion powder, and parsley on medium-low heat. Cook for 3 minutes, until the garlic mixture is fragrant but not browned.

Spread the asparagus in a single layer on the prepared pan. Lightly sprinkle with coarse sea salt and freshly ground pepper. Drizzle on the garlic-oil mixture.

Roast for 8-10 minutes, until the asparagus are bright green; do not overcook.

Transfer to a platter and serve hot.

Wild Rice with Mushrooms
(Recipe from Bon Appetit Magazine November 2001)

Ingredients:
8 tablespoons (1 stick) butter
4 large onions (about 2 3/4 pounds), halved, thinly sliced
1 1/4 pounds assorted wild mushrooms (such as crimini and stemmed shiitake), sliced
3 tablespoons chopped fresh thyme
5 cups canned low-salt chicken broth
3 teaspoons chopped fresh sage
1 1/3 cups wild rice (about one 8-ounce package)
1 1/4 cups long-grain white rice
1 3/4 cups coarsely chopped dried pears (about 7 ounces; optional)
3/4 to 1 cup chopped fresh Italian parsley
Add dried pears for subtle sweetness

Melt 4 tablespoons butter in heavy large pot over medium heat. Add onions; sauté until very tender and caramelized, about 25 minutes. Transfer onions to large bowl. Melt remaining 4 tablespoons butter in same pot over medium-high heat. Add mushrooms and 1 tablespoon thyme; sauté until mushrooms are deep brown, about 12 minutes. Add to bowl with onions. Season with salt and pepper.

Bring broth, 1 tablespoon thyme, and 2 teaspoons sage to boil in heavy large deep saucepan. Mix in wild rice; return to boil. Reduce heat; cover and simmer 30 minutes. Mix in white rice; cover and simmer until all rice is tender and almost all liquid is absorbed, about 18 minutes longer. Stir in caramelized onions and mushrooms, remaining 1 tablespoon thyme, and 1 teaspoon sage.

Stir in pears, if desired. Cover and simmer 5 minutes, stirring often. Season with salt and pepper. Stir in 3/4 cup parsley.

Flourless Chocolate Vanilla & Marble Cake
(by Abigail Johnson Dodge from Fine Cooking Issue 54)

For the vanilla batter:
8 oz. cream cheese, softened to room temperature
2/3 cup granulated sugar
1 large egg
1 tsp. pure vanilla extract

For the chocolate batter:
10 oz. bittersweet chocolate, finely chopped
5 oz. (10 Tbs.) unsalted butter, cut into 6 pieces
3 large eggs
1/3 cup granulated sugar

1 Tbs. dark rum or espresso
1 tsp. pure vanilla extract
Pinch table salt
Cocoa powder for dusting

TIP:
To slice the marble cake neatly, use a hot knife (run it
under hot running water and dry it). Wipe the blade
clean between slices.

Position an oven rack in the middle of the oven and
heat the oven to 300°F. Lightly grease a 9x2-inch round
cake pan and line the bottom with parchment.

Make the vanilla batter: In a medium bowl, beat the
softened cream cheese with an electric mixer until
smooth. Add the sugar and continue beating until well
blended and no lumps remain. Add the egg and vanilla
and beat just until blended. Set aside.

Make the chocolate batter: In a medium bowl, melt the
chocolate and butter in a large metal bowl over a pan
of simmering water or in the microwave. Whisk until
smooth and set aside to cool slightly. With a stand
mixer fitted with the whip attachment (or with a hand
mixer), beat the eggs, sugar, rum or espresso, vanilla,
and salt on medium high until the mixture is pale and
thick, 3 to 4 min. With the mixer on low, gradually
pour in the chocolate mixture and continue beating
until well blended.

Combine and bake: Spread about half of the chocolate
batter in the bottom of the pan. Alternately add large
scoopfuls of each of the remaining batters to the cake

pan. Using a knife or the tip of a rubber spatula, gently swirl the two batters together so they're mixed but not completely blended. Rap the pan against the countertop several times to settle the batters.

Bake until a pick inserted about 2 inches from the edge comes out gooey but not liquid, 40 to 42 min.; don't overbake. The top will be puffed and slightly cracked, especially around the edges. It will sink down as it cools. Let cool on a rack until just slightly warm, about 1-1/2 hours. Loosen the cake from the pan by holding the pan almost perpendicular to the counter; tap the pan on the counter while rotating it clockwise. Invert onto a large flat plate or board. Remove the pan and carefully peel off the parchment. Sift some cocoa powder over the cake (this will make it easier to remove the slices when serving). Invert again onto a similar plate so that the top side is up. Let cool completely. Cover and refrigerate until very cold, at least 4 hours or overnight, or freeze.

Notes

Chapter 1

[1] Naphtali Herz Imber, 1878, "Hatikvah," Wikipedia. Web

[2] Any Jewish Haggadah, the Four Questions

Chapter 2

[3] Lady Amelie Jacobovits, "Passover 1941,"aish.com," March 16, 2004, Web. August 5, 2014.

[4] Virginia Haynes, Testimony of a 2014 Passover Seder in Dallas, Texas

[5] Ruben Barrett, "How Do You Celebrate Passover" on Margaret Feinberg's Blog

[6] Dawn Zapata, "How Do You Celebrate Passover" on Margaret Feinberg's Blog

Chapter 3

[7] Any Jewish Haggadah

[8] A Family Haggadah II: A Seder Service for All Ages; by Shoshana Silberman; copyright 1987

[9] Margot R. Hodsons, "A Feast of Seasons: Passover Sacrificed for Us," hodsons.org/Afeastofseasons/id10.htm, Web.

Chapter 4

[10] Tim Chester, "A Meal With Jesus: Discovering Grace, Community & Mission around the Table," Crossway, Wheaton, Illinois, 2011, 118.

[11] Paul L. Maier, "In the Fullness of Time," Grand Rapids, MI Kregel Publications 1997, 128.

[12] Paul L. Maier, "In the Fullness of Time," Grand Rapids, MI Kregel Publications 1997, 126.

[13] NT Wright, *Jesus and the Victory of God* (Minneapolis: Fortress Press. 1996), 559

Chapter 5

[14] Devi Titus, "The Table Experience," Oviedo, FL, HigherLife Development Services, Inc., 2009, pg 43.

Chapter 6

[15] Beth Moore, "The Patriarchs," Nashville, TN, Lifeway Press, Fourth Printing 2005, 81.

Chapter 7

[16] Any Jewish Haggadah

[17] John F. Walvoord and Roy B. Zuck, "The Bible Knowledge Commentary: Old Testament," Colorado Springs, CO, David C Cook, 1984, 812.

[18] Ruth Spector Lascelle, "The Passover Feast," Van Nuys, CA, Ruth Spector Lascelle, 1990, 28.

Chapter 8

[19] Tim Chester, "A Meal With Jesus: Discovering Grace, Community & Mission around the Table," Crossway, Wheaton, Illinois, 2011, 121.

Chapter 9

[20] Any Jewish Haggadah

[21] Zola Levitt, "The Miracle of Passover," Zola Levitt, 1977, 22, 23.

[22] Tim Chester, "A Meal With Jesus: Discovering Grace, Community & Mission around the Table," Crossway, Wheaton, Illinois, 2011, 117.

Chapter 10

[23] Any Jewish Haggadah

Chapter 11

[24] Shauna Niequest, "Bread & Wine: A Love Letter To Life Around The Table With Recipes," Zondervan, Grand Rapids, MI, 2013, 40.

[25] Tim Chester, "A Meal With Jesus: Discovering Grace, Community & Mission around the Table," Crossway, Wheaton, Illinois, 2011, 12.

About the Authors

Melanie Leach lives in North Dallas and is originally from South Louisiana. She graduated from Nicholls State University, and has been a marketer for the past twenty years, most recently at PepsiCo's Frito Lay North America's Strategic Innovation Marketing division. She has always been interested in and curious about Christianity's Jewish roots and heritage. She and her husband have led Christian Passover Seders for many years in their home with co-workers, friends and neighbors. These Passover dinners sparked wonderful conversation around the table and ignited a passion to bring this experience to others.

Melanie and her husband of ten years, Will, are foodies and enjoy cooking and entertaining friends and neighbors. They have a five-year-old son, Nicholas, who keeps them on their toes.

Susie Hawkins lives in Dallas and has been actively involved in ministry as a pastor's wife, teacher and volunteer. She has served as the Director of Women's Ministry at Prestonwood Baptist Church and currently speaks at various women's conferences and events. She has an MA in Theology from The Criswell College, is a contributor to various publications, and is on the writing team for Flourish, a website designed for ministry wives. She is the author of "From One Ministry Wife to Another".

Susie enjoys traveling to Israel with her husband, O.S., and exploring Christianity's Jewish roots and its rich history. She has participated in Seders while in Florida, Texas and Israel and wants others to share in these valuable insights and discoveries. Susie and OS have two married daughters and six young grandchildren who have joined her discovering why Passover is "a night that is different from any other night."

Please visit www.PassoverforChristians.com for more information and tools to conduct your own Passover Seder this season.

Made in the USA
San Bernardino, CA
26 February 2019